Grandparents
ILLINOIS STYLE

by Mike Link and Kate Crowley

Adventure Publications, Inc.
Cambridge, Minnesota

Dedication:

To Matthew, Aren, Ryan and Annalise, who have taught us the magic of grandparenting.

Photo credits:

Cover and book design by Jonathan Norberg

10 9 8 7 6 5 4 3 2 1

Published by Adventure Publications, Inc.
820 Cleveland St. S
Cambridge, MN 55008
1-800-678-7006
www.adventurepublications.net
Printed in China
ISBN-13: 978-1-59193-172-0
ISBN-10: 1-59193-172-X

Contents

Introduction 6

A Word from Mike Link 8

A Word from Kate Crowley 10

How to Use This Book 11

Map 12

Adler Planetarium & Astronomy Museum 14

American Girl Place 16

Biking in Chicago 18

Chicago Air & Water Show 20

The Art Institute of Chicago 22

Chicago Children's Museum & Kohl Children's Museum 24

The Field Museum 26

Lincoln Park Zoo 28

John G. Shedd Aquarium 30

The Peggy Notebaert Nature Museum .32

Millennium Park 34

Museum of Science and Industry 36

Touch the Sky 38

Wrigley Field 40

Chicago Botanic Garden 42

Spring Valley Nature Sanctuary & Volkening Heritage Farm 44

Ravinia Festival 46

Volo Bog State Natural Area 48

Illinois Railway Museum 50

Discovery Center Museum & Burpee Museum of Natural History 52

Anderson Japanese Gardens 54

Brookfield Zoo 56

Midewin National Tallgrass Prairie &
Goose Lake Prairie State Natural Area 58

I & M Canal and Great River Trails 60

Ulysses S. Grant Home 62

National Mississippi River Museum & Aquarium 64

Rock Island Arsenal Museum 66

Quad City Botanical Center 68

John Deere Pavilion 70

Bishop Hill 72

Nauvoo 74

Wildlife Prairie State Park 76

Miller Park 78

Lincoln's New Salem State Historic Site 80

Lincoln Home National Historic Site 82

Illinois State Capitol 84

Illinois State Museum 86

Abraham Lincoln Presidential Library and Museum 88

Chanute Aerospace Museum 90

Wandell Sculpture Garden 92

Amish Country: Arthur and Arcola 94

Raggedy Ann & Andy Museum and Festival 96

National Great Rivers Museum 98

Lewis and Clark State Historic Site 100

Cahokia Mounds State Historic Site 102

Tunnel Hill State Trail 104

Garden of the Gods 106

Cypress Creek National Wildlife Refuge 108

Seeking Superman 110

Fort Massac State Park 112

Bald Eagles and the Rivers 114

Canoeing 116

Illinois Weather 118

City Parks 120

Cooking Together 122

State Parks 124

Fireworks 126

Kite Flying 128

Grandparents Day 130

Picnicking 132

Hot Air Balloon Ride 134

Lake Michigan Beaches 136

Fishing 138

Gardening 140

Amtrak 142

Campfire 144

The Land of Poetry 146

Cemetery Visit 148

Farmers' Market 150

Library 152

Nature Centers 154

Index 156

About the Authors 160

Introduction

Grandparents Illinois Style is for today's grandparents who want to spend more time discovering the world with their grandchildren. This book is about opportunities for adults and children to have fun, laugh and share. Of course, Illinois is ripe with more possibilities than we can cover, but this is a place to get started. We decided to write this book because of our experiences with our grandchildren—three boys and a girl. They provide us with a lot of fun, but we also have a responsibility to them. We can use our time together to help them learn and grow as individuals.

In writing this book we've had to stop and think about the knowledge we've gained, how we learned valuable life lessons and how we could pass our wisdom to our grandchildren. With the changing times, we found that several experiences have become endangered—solitude, silence, open space, dark night skies, free time, reading books and home-cooked food.

Consider the following changes:

1. Farms are no longer a part of most children's experiences. In 1900, farmers accounted for forty percent of our census. By 1990, the total fell below two percent.

2. Open space was once a playground. Now it is slated for development. Children are left with only fenced yards and indoor locations.

3. The "out in the country" experience is disappearing. Urban sprawl means an hour's drive from the inner city to any country areas.

4. Tree climbing is more difficult now. There are few open areas of trees for Jacks and Jills to climb magic beanstalks.

5. The chance to be bored—which is an opportunity to be creative—isn't often in the schedule. Children are signed up for every organized activity and training available, eliminating family time and free time.

6. Sports used to be for fun. Now some parents have children choose a sport, then send them to summer camps where winning is what matters.

7. Canning, pickling and baking—all of those wonderful activities that filled the root-cellars and pantries of the past—are less common.

Today's world has seen some bad and dangerous trends. Fast food (and obesity) is the norm. Meth and other deadly drugs flood our cities, our neighborhoods and our schools.

Fortunately, our grandchildren have us. The role of the grandparent can be different than it was when we were kids, and we can adapt, too. Grandparents have many opportunities:

1. Grandparents are living longer than ever before and can influence their grandchildren longer.

2. Parents work long days, filled with busy hours.

3. Grandparents can provide children with quiet times, new experiences and more play.

4. Grandparents can help introduce children to healthy food; we have the time to prepare it and present it.

5. Children may gain from perspectives other than those of their peers and they may benefit from our guidance and insight.

We may be able to involve the extended family in more activities and be part of the new modern family of the twenty-first century.

That's not to say we should take on the role of mother and father. Instead our place is to supplement a child's parents, to help them wherever our help is wanted and needed. Let's use the time we have with our grandchildren to instill in them important values, to teach them about the world around them and to help shape them into better people.

A Word from Mike Link

"Where are you, Dad?"

"We got a late start and have about an hour until we get to you, why?"

"Well you better hurry. Your grandson heard Gampa was coming and now we're sitting out on the curb waiting for you to arrive."

An hour later we found our greeting party on the curb, on the blanket. Who could ask for a better welcome than that? That's the love our grandchildren have for us if we are willing to involve ourselves in their lives, the reason we want to create special memories with our grandchildren. Our greatest gift to them is our love and attention. They are the greatest gift we could receive.

What ancestors gave us:

The role of the grandparent is significant and has played an important part in my life, Kate's life and the lives of our children. I spent all of my "non-school" time living with my grandparents in Rice Lake, Wisconsin, while my father worked evenings and weekends to try to get us out of the poverty that surrounded us. I was born in Rice Lake. My father and mother moved to Minnesota for work, but in spirit they never really left Wisconsin.

My dad worked second shift, from 3 p.m. to midnight, and that meant we had little time together, so my grandfather taught me to play catch, to drive, to work. He was my partner. My grandmother picked berries with me, taught me the pleasure of fresh-baked pies and cookies. Both of them were there to guide me, to share with me, and to set an example.

I was also lucky to know my great grandparents and to see my heritage through them. It was a wonderful way to connect time and generations. In some ways it was a tradition begun before I came along. My great-great-grandmother, Ogima Benisi Kwe (Chief Bird Woman) was from the La Court O'Reilles reservation; she married my great-great-grandfather John Quaderer, fresh from Liechtenstein. He had entered the country through New Orleans, come up the Mississippi, and ended up in the Chippewa River Valley.

Their daughter, Anna Kahl, my great-grandmother, was a wonderful woman who raised not only her thirteen children on their Prairie Farm farm, but also five of my uncles who moved back to the reservation as they reached adulthood. She carried forward the tradition that a grandparent should be the role model and the teacher, while the parents provide safety, home, food and other provisions. She is part of who I am, part of my connection with the world.

My grandmother Prock's kolaches were the connection to our Czech heritage. Sauerkraut, roast pork and mashed potatoes were an extension of our German heritage. My Anishanabe heritage created the succession of grandparent/grandchild roles and bonds that continue today. I believe that the role of the traditional grandparent is one that fits today's needs.

What we can give grandchildren:

Our society has caused some parents to allow others to "coach" their children into maturity. This may not be the parent's choice, but the demands to make a living are great.

Do not despair; there is a solution that is ancient. In a *Washington Post* editorial Abigail Trafford describes the plight of today's families; she refers to the next two decades as the transition from baby boomers to grand baby boomers.

Today grandparents live longer, have the potential for better health and more opportunities than ever before to share their stories, read books, look at old photo albums, talk about the good old days and enjoy their grandchildren. But what to do? Talking, reading and photo albums are all great, but the stories are wonderful because you lived them, the photos have meaning because you experienced something that the photo reminds you of.

If you want to build memories rather than dwelling on them, get out, get going, take those grandchildren and experience the world again for the first time through their smiles, their curiosity, their energy.

In, *Contemporary Grandparenting*, 1996, Arthur Kornhaber, M.D., shows the evolution of individuals from their own childhood to grandparenting:

- from receiving as a child to giving as an elder
- from being nurtured as a child to nurturing the young
- from learning to teaching
- from listening to stories to telling them
- from being directed to directing
- from simply reacting to one's environment to becoming able to influence the world
- from identifying with others to becoming an object of identification

We are the elders; we are the starting point for more generations. How exciting and how challenging. But don't dwell on responsibility. Just be yourself. Be honest, be fun, be open. Grandchildren are gifts from the future and through them we can see the decades ahead—they connect us to their world and we give them a connection to ours.

A Word from Kate Crowley

If you're lucky, you grew up knowing your grandparents. If you're even luckier those grandparents lived nearby and enriched your life by their interest and enthusiastic involvement. Unfortunately, the Industrial Revolution, while it has brought us lives of relative ease and abundance, has also brought about the decline of the close-knit, extended family.

Much of the knowledge that our grandparents carried was tied to life on the land. We can recall the easy times spent with these adults who indulged us and shared their memories of a time that today seems remote. Yet, since we carry the memories and experiences with us, we have the opportunity to share them with a new generation, being born into a century with untold opportunities and far too many dangers.

As we age, we reflect on our childhoods. Even though time tends to spray a cloud of gold over those days, we know there were experiences that gave us great pleasure and cemented the bonds with the grandparents who shared themselves with us.

When I was born, I had two living grandmothers. One lived in California, and I have very fuzzy memories of her. She visited us only a handful of times, and I don't recall her as particularly warm or even interested in interacting with my siblings or me.

My other grandmother lived just a block away from us, and I had more than twenty years of close acquaintance with her. I even lived with her for four years during and after high school. She didn't have the time or personality to get down on the floor and play with us, but her house was always open to us and we wore a path through our neighbors' backyards to get there. She had a few old toys and books for us to play with and a big, old piano that we made noise on, but mostly we came over to visit. If we were lucky, she'd make us root beer floats.

Memories of time with our grandparents are tied to our senses, all of which were much keener as children. Smell, sight, sound, touch and taste—these are the things that will stay with children as they grow to adulthood, recalling times shared with grandparents.

One of the most mouth-watering, sensual memories I have of my grandmother is from a summer day, when we went out into the country to pick tomatoes. It was a hot day and even though we got there early, the sun was beating down on us as we moved through the rows of pungent tomatoes. What I remember most about the day is that she packed cheese sandwiches—most likely Velveeta—and I have never eaten anything more delicious than a rich, sweet tomato right off the vine, still holding the sun's heat, juice running down my chin, followed by a bite of soft cheese on white bread. The smells and tastes flowed together, and I can see us there now, joined forever by this act of harvesting food.

I have waited a very long time to become a grandmother and not just because our daughters chose to wait until their thirties to have children. I can't explain why, but even when my two children were preteens, I was contemplating grandparenthood. I packed away all of their Fisher Price toys in the original boxes to share with the next generation, and I saved as many of their books as possible. I so greatly enjoyed raising those two children that I knew I wanted to have similar experiences again—but without the many worries and day-to-day concerns of parenthood. I understood even then that, as a grandparent, I would be able to have fun, play, act silly and share what I've learned but still have the luxury of going home at the end of the day to a quiet, clean house.

Now we have three grandsons and one granddaughter—all of whom arrived within the span of four years—and we are looking forward to years of adventures together. This is why we've written *Grandparents Illinois Style*: to help other grandparents find those unique and unforgettable places that will combine fun and facts, history and humor, excitement and enduring memories for you and for the special grandchildren in your life.

How to Use This Book

The suggestions in this book are just that: suggestions. Some experiences are unmatchable anywhere else in the state. Others can be replicated. If you are not near the museum, park or site that we highlight, find a similar place near you. Read our suggestions and pay special attention to each "Bonding and bridging" to tie your visit to an important life lesson.

We do not advocate that you become the "wallet" or the "chauffeur." What we want you to consider is an active participation in friendship and sharing that is enriched by love. We want you to receive the respect due an elder, to share your experience and to enjoy the love that can flow between generations.

One of the themes of this book is that things change. This is true for everything, including the state's attractions. They sometimes close, renovate or move. When in doubt, *CALL BEFORE YOU LEAVE HOME*.

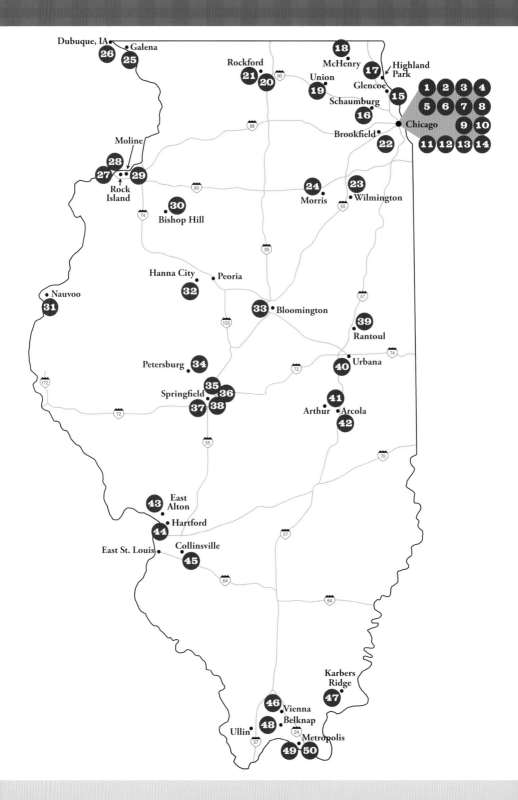

The sites appear in the book in the order below, beginning with those in Chicago and the northwestern part of the state and proceeding southward.

SITE NUMBER		PAGE NUMBER
1	Adler Planetarium & Astronomy Museum	14
2	American Girl Place	16
3	Biking in Chicago	18
4	Chicago Air & Water Show	20
5	The Art Institute of Chicago	22
6	Chicago Children's Museum & Kohl's Children's Museum	24
7	The Field Museum	26
8	Lincoln Park Zoo	28
9	John G. Shedd Aquarium	30
10	The Peggy Notebaert Nature Museum	32
11	Millennium Park	34
12	Museum of Science and Industry	36
13	Touch the Sky	38
14	Wrigley Field	40
15	Chicago Botanic Garden	42
16	Spring Valley Nature Sanctuary & Volkening Heritage Farm	44
17	Ravinia Festival	46
18	Volo Bog State Natural Area	48
19	Illinois Railway Museum	50
20	Discovery Center Museum & Burpee Museum of Natural History	52
21	Anderson Japanese Gardens	54
22	Brookfield Zoo	56
23	Midewin National Tallgrass Prairie & Goose Lake Prairie State Natural Area	58
24	I & M Canal State Trail and Great River Trails	60
25	Ulysses S. Grant Home	62

SITE NUMBER		PAGE NUMBER
26	National Mississippi River Museum & Aquarium	64
27	Rock Island Arsenal Museum	66
28	Quad City Botanical Center	68
29	John Deere Pavilion	70
30	Bishop Hill	72
31	Nauvoo	74
32	Wildlife Prairie State Park	76
33	Miller Park	78
34	Lincoln's New Salem State Historic Site	80
35	Lincoln Home National Historic Site	82
36	Illinois State Capitol	84
37	Illinois State Museum	86
38	Abraham Lincoln Presidential Library and Museum	88
39	Chanute Aerospace Museum	90
40	Wandell Sculpture Garden	92
41	Amish Country: Arthur and Arcola	94
42	Raggedy Ann & Andy Museum and Festival	96
43	National Great Rivers Museum	98
44	Lewis and Clark State Historic Site	100
45	Cahokia Mounds State Historic Site	102
46	Tunnel Hill State Trail	104
47	Garden of the Gods	106
48	Cypress Creek National Wildlife Refuge	108
49	Seeking Superman	110
50	Fort Massac State Park	112

Statewide activities start on page 114

Adler Planetarium & Astronomy Museum

Where can you go that would beat traveling through the solar system or the universe? Could you go anywhere with your grandchild that would be more unforgettable? Of course tickets for such trips are quite expensive, unless you book your passage at the Adler Planetarium. The planetarium includes the Sky Theater Show, the Astronomy Museum and the StarRider Theater.

This is a museum, an exploration, a journey. Get tickets for the Sky Theater Shows—they change regularly so you can take a different trip each time you return. The Sky Theater is different from the surrounding museum and also different from the StarRider Theater. The Sky Theater is like a magnificent telescope that can encompass the entire night sky. Here you can explore the stars and the legends that have grown around their shapes and clusters. As you take a seat, the auditorium darkens and the sky appears. Specters of light begin to form on the circular screen as music, movement, and images coalesce and take you to the far reaches of space without the pressure of additional G forces or the discomfort of a small capsule.

At the StarRider Theater you can choose from a variety of virtual reality offerings that might include the exploration of black holes, or even time travel. Be adventurous and commit part of your visit to these opportunities and then enjoy the interactive exhibits. Nothing in the Adler is boring, as the museum incorporates hands-on experience. You can take a 3-D journey through the Milky Way or drive a rover through the solar system when you sit down at the computer and take over the controls. One exhibit explores the growth of human knowledge from the time when people thought our little planet was the center of the universe. Sundials, astrolabes, and spheres help us gain a perspective on those early periods, while the exhibit on space exploration allows us to imagine our future adventures. And the cyberspace exhibit helps the children make a more direct connection with the open vistas of space. And if that is not enough, you can enjoy the Chicago skyline from Galileo's café, or the America's Courtyard sculpture that captures the spirit of Stonehenge, and all the famous astronomical structures of the ancient world. The Infinity Shop sells some very high quality merchandise designed to help you remember your adventure after you leave.

Bonding and bridging:

Our grandparents were born into an age of horse and buggy. They thrilled to the news of Orville Wright's short flight and lived to see not only cars and planes, but a landing on the moon. Our parents were thrilled by Lindbergh's flight to Paris and the tragedy of Amelia Earhart's disappearance over the Pacific Ocean. We have shared the excitement of the moon landing, jets that carry us all over the world, and the Hubble telescope.

We remember Kennedy's challenge and the landing on the moon, the terrible loss of life in the history of our space program, and the wonderful new vistas of distant rocks and landscapes. Now our grandchildren come into a world that expects to travel into space. Let your grandchildren know about the space race and then wonder at what our grandchildren will see.

A word to the wise:

This is the home of the Doane Observatory, a real telescope that is available to the public every "Far Out Friday" and on special occasions. Your grandchildren will be impressed with this large scope that can gather over 5000 times the light that an unaided human eye can gather! Its 20-inch (0.5 m) diameter mirror lets visitors see celestial objects like the moon, planets, stars, and galaxies that are beyond our range of vision.

Age of grandchild: 8 and up

Best season: All

Contact: Adler Planetarium and Museums, 1300 South Lake Shore Drive, Chicago, IL 60605 • (312) 922-STAR • http://www.adlerplanetarium.org

Also check out:

William M Staerkel Planetarium, Parkland College, Champaign; (217) 351-2568; (217) 351-2446 (show hotline); www.parkland.edu/planetarium/

Lakeview Museum, Peoria; (309) 686-7000; www.lakeview-museum.org

American Girl Place

It might seem strange that we are including the American Girl Place in this guide, and it's true this is a place where people buy things, but if handled right it can be a highlight of a little girl's trip. If you spend time preparing for the first visit, it may be a magical moment.

I was never a girl who loved dolls. As the oldest of seven, there always seemed to be a new baby in the house. Who needed an inanimate toy to play with

when there was a living one in the next room? My daughter loved dolls and now that we have a granddaughter, I have begun to plan a special excursion for us when she is seven years old.

Preparation: Before we make this trip, we are going to read some books about girls who lived in this country in different eras, beginning in 1774, up until the 1970s. What makes the American Girl doll unique are the nine main historical characters (with four additional friends) included in this series of the American Girl books. Written by contemporary authors, some award-winning, the stories detail the challenges these girls face in their lives. Many of the challenges cross time and culture, such as loyalty, bravery, empathy, creativity, a sense of humor and independence—all qualities we'd like our granddaughters to acquire. These stories can also make history seem relevant and interesting.

Step Two: I hope Annalise will choose one of the characters who speaks to her own sense of self (I already have my personal favorite, but I will try to keep that to myself) and then we will plan our adventure to get her doll.

Step Three: The store itself is a monument to girls. Pink is the predominant color and there are three floors dedicated to fulfilling the young girl's fantasy. The street level holds a bookstore and photo studio. The second level has a doll hospital and hair salon, as well as the Café. The lower level has a theater and glass fronted exhibits.

Bonding and bridging:

Planning a visit to the "American Girl Place" can be half the fun. Certainly, you will want to tell her about the favorite doll you had as a child.

At the store, you can include a tea or another meal in the Café or you can buy tickets to one of their live theatrical presentations. There are special events around the holidays and there are even some special "Great Day with a Grandparent" events throughout the year.

Once your granddaughter has her doll, encourage her to write her own stories for her 'girl'. You can participate in this process by reading stories together from the time period the doll represents. And for a few short years, the three of you will share adventures and fun together.

A word to the wise:

This experience can only succeed with the cooperation of the parents. Get their approval first, of course, and then ask whether you and your granddaughter can make this excursion personal and special. It is probably impossible to visit American Girl Place without making a purchase of some kind—the temptations are just too great, so it will also be important to set a dollar limit before you go to avoid pouting or whining. Check their website to get a sense of the price range you're willing and able to cover and then let your granddaughter decide before the trip how she will spend that allotment.

Age of grandchild: 4 to 10

Best season: All

Contact: American Girl Place, 111 East Chicago Avenue, Chicago, IL 60611 • (877) 247-5223 • www.americangirl.com

Also check out:

Raggedy Ann & Andy Museum; (217) 268-4908; www.raggedyann-museum.org/

Wheels O' Time Museum, Peoria; (309) 243-9020; www.wheelsotime.org

Illinois Farm Toy Show; http://www.toyfarmer.com/events/

Even now, I am not old. I never think of it, and yet I am a grandmother to eleven grandchildren. GRANDMA MOSES

Biking in Chicago

Learning to ride a bike can be harrowing and frustrating for a child, but once they get it, the world opens up in wonderful ways. Distances grow shorter and the speed feels exhilarating. And, fortunately, once you learn how, your body remembers, so we can ride well into our old age—even if it is slower and for shorter distances. Biking remains a great means of exploring and making discoveries.

Chicago offers many means of getting around—buses, trolleys, subways, the El, carriages, taxis, and on foot. But for the older grandchild, with energy bursting from every pore, a bicycle ride is probably the best "ticket." We recommend joining a guided bike tour, from one of several local companies. There are lakefront tours, neighborhood tours, and even nighttime rides, most of which are concentrated in areas close to the Lake Shore where there are over 18 miles of trails.

The guides are well versed in the history and sights of the city, and they are also very safety conscious. Most of the rides last 2-3 hours and cover approximately six miles, so they are leisurely paced. Bikes and helmets are provided. Reservations are usually required, especially during busy tourist times.

And if you are adventurous, but have a younger, less proficient grandchild, there are a variety of choices. You can rent a tandem; a two wheeled wagon that attaches behind your bike; child seats; or something called a tagalong, which is like half a bike that attaches under the seat of your bike. That way the child can feel as though they are riding too, even though you are doing most of the work and steering. If balance is an issue, there are the quadcycles, which look a bit like a horseless buggy. They offer more stability and can seat up to 4 people.

If you feel confident of your navigational skills in the city and don't like to travel in packs, or you don't have time for a full tour, you can create your own tour itinerary and have a safe, fun biking experience on the trails along the lakeshore.

Bonding and bridging:

Whether you were around to help your grandchild learn to ride a bike or not, sharing a biking adventure like this is sure to create long lasting memories for both of you. Grandchildren may be surprised and amused that even at your advanced age you can still pedal and you will find pleasure in their skills and endless energy. Riding side by side you can talk with them about your first bike and how you learned to ride and how much you used your bike in those ancient days of one-car families.

A word to the wise:

You must be a judge of your grandchild's personality and patience for the stops and mini-lectures by the guides and their attention to safety. Be sure to bring water, especially on those warm summer days, and drink it. Once you become dehydrated it is hard for the body to recover no matter how much liquid you pour down your throat. In addition, a little energy food in your pack would be good. Children tend to run full tilt and then crash. When the child's energy runs out so does their good mood, patience, and good behavior and the same might be true for the grandparents! Finally, make sure you wear your helmet, setting a good example.

Age of grandchild: 3 and up

Best season: Spring, summer and fall

Contact:

Bobby's Bike Hike, Ogden Slip at River East Docks, 465 North McClurg Court, Chicago, IL 60610 • (312) 915-0995 • www.bobbysbikehike.com

Bike Chicago Rentals and Tours, Navy Pier/Millennium Park/North Avenue Beach/Riverwalk/Foster Avenue Beach • www.bikechicago.com

McDonald's Cycle Center, 239 East Randolph Street, Chicago IL 60601 (888) 245-3929 • www.chicagobikestation.com

Also check out:

Illinois DNR bicycling guide
http://dnr.state.il.us/Lands/Landmgt/Programs/Biking/bikegde.htm

I like to walk with Grandpa, his steps are short like mine.
He doesn't say, "Now hurry up." He always takes his time. Unknown

Chicago Air & Water Show

In a city that thrives on the skyscraper image, a city that seems to rise from the waters of Lake Michigan into the clouds, the annual Air and Water Show seems like the perfect community celebration. Started in 1959 as a part of "family days," this celebration has become an historic tradition ideal for all ages.

People arrive early and line the beaches for this August event. North Avenue Beach is the central focus of both the flights and the water show, but you

can get great views from Oak Street Beach, the south part of Lincoln Park, or Olive Park as well. This is a free weekend event and a great time to celebrate, observe, and share.

The air will be filled with famous flying teams that range from the military precision teams like the Thunderbirds to brightly colored biplanes. The planes soar and roar in formations that seem unbelievable at the speeds they're traveling. The jets, moving at great speeds, set up wonderful views of both skyline and airplanes. Less speedy and powerful, the older planes may spiral upward, then set themselves into free fall, with smoke released to emphasize the seemingly out-of-control plunge towards earth. Others perform ballet and gymnastic stunts with grace and imagination.

Bring cameras and binoculars to watch the events. In addition to the planes, you and the grandchildren will want to watch the wild aviators do tricks on the wings of the old planes and the daredevils come out of the sky attached to colorful parachutes.

Then, if you can take your eyes off the wild blue yonder, you will want to look out at the blue horizon and see the show on the water. Fast boats, water-skiers, wake boarders, and wave riders provide wet thrills and excitement.

The crowds are large—North Beach will fill first, and there are no places to sit or get shade unless you plan ahead. Bring a little cooler, umbrellas, and lots of patience—it will be worth it.

Bonding and bridging:

There is something exciting and frightening about the display of military might and power. The Air Show should be about enjoying the spectacle and then talking about what you saw. Mike's grandfather went from horse and buggy to car to plane to the moon landing in his lifetime. A bicycle maker's discovery has led to modern aviation and stealth bombers and helicopters. Share stories of your first trip in an airplane. Talk about the good things planes have done for us, but also share how lucky we are to never have seen planes like these flying over our cities in real combat. Our freedom and way of life have been built upon a balance of diplomacy and military preparedness and as citizens of the future, your grandchildren need to understand the value of both.

A word to the wise:

Young children may have trouble following all the action. The jets are especially difficult because they cover large areas at great speed and seem to disappear and reappear without warning. The older planes and the water show will be much easier. Give them some help—remember that the jets sound trails the plane so they must learn to look ahead of the sound. For the younger ones, the roar of the planes may be frightening. Better to leave, if that's the case and save the show for another year. In addition, bring sunscreen and an umbrella—this is August and sunburns will not provide a good ending to a great day.

Age of grandchild: 4 and up

Best season: August

Contact: Chicago Air and Water Show, North Beach, Lincoln Park and all the waterfront from the Navy Pier north • (312) 744-3315
www.chicagoairandwatershow.us

Also check out:

Springfield Air Rendezvous, Springfield; (217) 789-4400; www.springfield-il.com/airshow

Chanute Aerospace Museum, Rantoul; (217) 893-1613; www.aeromuseum.org

When grandparents enter the door, discipline flies out the window. Ogden Nash

The Art Institute of Chicago

The giant stairs lead up to the columns and doors of the art institute. The lions stand in vigilance, silently testing each person who passes. Some people might be intimidated and walk on by. But the lucky ones, like you, can see this wonderful setting as an entrance to alternate universes, time travel, shifting perspectives, and human creativity. For those who enter the bustling interior and steps that seem to go in random ways, it is an adventure.

An art institute need not be imposing, it should be fun. Start in the basement with your grandchildren. There is a classroom where you might use your own

creativity, a touch room where you are asked to touch the statues and a room of miniatures that look like they came out of the most elaborate and beautiful doll houses ever created.

This grand facility started in 1879 as both a school and a museum. Built on the remains of the Chicago Fire of 1871, it can literally claim to have risen from the ashes. The museum started with personal gifts and daring vision that soon filled the first building. But there was much more art to claim and display, so the museum just expanded right over the active railroad tracks that had been out their back door.

Now there are classic art works from around the world, imaginative imagery in sculpture, paint, photography, glass, wood, minerals, and metals. Some will shock, some will puzzle, and some will cause you to smile. These are all forms of the human emotions and you can allow yourself the gift of liking, disliking, and even laughing at various pieces.

If your grandchildren like the fantasy and adventure stories of Harry Potter and the Knights of the Round Table, spend time with them in the hall of knights and armor. It's hard for any of us to look at these without a visit in our minds from King Arthur, and that is what art is all about.

Bonding and bridging:

All kids like to color and as we grow up we draw, play music, quilt, needlepoint, build in the woodshop, restore or customize cars, enjoy films, take photos, build sand castles and create new ideas. All of this is art, but we don't label it that way. Instead people think art is something foreign, something for the "high brow." But look around at the posters for concerts, films, church dinners—we use illustration and art to tell our stories. Share a favorite children's book, like *Where the Wild Things Are*, and see how the art creates the scary feelings. Perhaps teach them to pay attention to names of the illustrators. Pictures in books are art, too.

A word to the wise:

Just remember there is too much art to see in any one visit. Look as long as it is fun and come back another day. There is no rule that says you have to see everything in the museum. Nothing can spoil the desire to return more than boredom. See the things that spark interest, avoid those that don't. Pick special shows you know will interest them and take them when they are ready.

Age of grandchild: all ages

Best season: All year, but rainy days or bad weather make this a great escape

Contact: Chicago Art Institute, 111 South Michigan Avenue, Chicago, IL, 60603 • (312) 443-3600 • www.artic.edu

Also check out:

Illinois State Museum, Springfield; (217) 782-7386; www.museum.state.il.us

Elmhurst Art Museum, Elmhurst; (630) 834-0202; www.elmhurstartmuseum.org

Rockford Art Museum, Rockford; (815) 968-2787; www.rockfordartmuseum.org

McLean County Arts Center, Bloomington; (309) 829-0011; www.mcac.org

Contemporary Art Center, Peoria; http://peoriacac.org/

Lakewood Museum of Arts and Science, Peoria; www.lakeview-museum.org

One way to open your eyes is to ask yourself, "What if I had never seen this before? What if I knew I would never see it again?" RACHEL CARSON

Chicago Children's Museum & Kohl Children's Museum

In the midst of shops, ships, and stores there is a bonanza of kid friendly activities to discover at the Children's Museum at the Navy Pier. This is where grandparent becomes guide, counselor, and instigator, to guide them through, letting the child's imagination make the choices, while you watch over safety and the possible conflict that can arise from lots of little hands and feet concentrating on the same objects. Keep them playing. Help them avoid competition and conflict by directing them to what they can do.

There are three floors of creativity and a cargo net passage way that will challenge the children and allow you to see their progress. In the Kovler Family Climbing Schooner, the kids go from the aquariums in the depth of the sea to the crow's nest on the upper floor. Then to settle down the adrenaline, go to the Inventing Lab and turn their energy into constructive activities that allow them to express their imagination. Or go to the BIG Backyard where

they can move through the oversized garden and play among the toadstools and insects, giggling flowers and oversized experiences. There are Treehouse Trails and Kids Town and a variety of changing exhibits that keeps this space active and filled with surprises.

Should you want to avoid the bustle and crowds of the Navy Pier you have other options in Chicago and perhaps the best is the new Kohl Children's Museum in Glenview, with both inside and outside creative areas.

The Kohl has a wonderful "store" where children learn about buying groceries and mimic the tasks that they have seen their parents do. They also have a fun construction zone where they can learn about building. The indoor activities are outstanding and varied, but the outdoor options are a unique and important place for children to learn to play.

Prepare to get wet, even if it is only your grandchild playing, because the water exhibits are too much fun for the children to avoid getting involved. Bring extra clothes.

Bonding and bridging:

In play, the child also looks for approval, and grandparents are ideal candidates to encourage, praise, and offer inspiration. The grandparent needs to allow the child to have the experience— that means stepping back, letting the child explore.

Help them learn to pace themselves (a very tough task) and process the things they learn. "How did that . . . work?" "What did you like best and why?"

A word to the wise:

This is your day to enable and observe. Take advantage of programs where the staff helps children create objects, using art and focusing their energies and inspiration. You will want to slow down and let the children engage fully. When it feels overwhelming, suggest that Grandpa or Grandma is a little tired and if they will go to one of the quiet areas with you and relax a while, they can stay even longer.

Age of grandchild: Up to age 10 seems perfect

Best season: All

Contact:

Chicago Children's Museum, 700 East Grand Avenue, #127, Chicago, IL 60611 • (312) 527-1000 • www.chicagochildrensmuseum.org

Kohl Children's Museum, Glenview; (847) 832-6600; www.kohlchildrensmuseum.org

Also check out:

Bronzeville Children's Museum, Chicago; (773) 721-9301; www.bronzevillechildrensmuseum.com/index1.html

Chain O'Lakes Area Artworks Children's Museum, Ingleside; (847) 587-7882; www.artworks4kids.org

DuPage Children's Museum, Naperville; (630) 637-8000; www.dupagechildrensmuseum.org

Health World Children's Museum, Barrington; (847) 842-9100; www.healthworldoutreach.org

One hundred years from now, it will not matter what my bank account was, how big my house was, or what kind of car I drove. But the world may be a little better because I was important in the life of a child. FOREST WITCRAFT

The Field Museum

This is an old building, large, imposing, and filled with mysteries that we can hardly begin to imagine. Going into the Field Museum is like opening a treasure chest that Mother Nature has filled. When the lid is off, the collection is so dazzling and so immense that we can hardly comprehend the contents.

Our grandson, a month short of his fourth birthday, went to the evolving earth exhibit and enjoyed some parts, especially pushing all the buttons. The centerpiece is an exhibit of many reconstructed dinosaurs and this was exciting. After

getting used to bone creatures, our grandson did found it intriguing but he enjoyed the "What is an Animal" exhibit much more.

Talk about wonderful exhibits. Colors and designs mix in ways that emphasize the diversity of the natural world. It is a story that is wonderfully told and works on many levels even for very young children. The "Nature Walk" was a great complement with animals our grandson recognized in well-done habitat settings. "Underground World" was effective, but a little too hard for a very young child to grasp.

The "Plant World" is another step up for children, most of whom do not think about plants in the exciting way that they do animals. The rocks are more effective if you choose the stories you spend time at. The examples are terrific.

"Traveling the World and Seeing Other Cultures" is another great story, so large that it would be best to see it in another visit. It is easy to look at so many exhibits that you become dazed and really do not take in the details. Those aspects that emphasize jewelry and various crafts are less interesting to the young so you need to be selective about where you spend your time.

If you are not comfortable with the large variety of exhibits and stories, you can do some preparation before your visit by visiting their website. The site offers downloadable self-guided tours like the "Scavenger Hunt." They also have family adventures that help you observe the details within the exhibit that link the information to a coherent storyline. This is a wonderful way to discover and learn together.

Bonding and bridging:

Unlike animals in a zoo, these animals are dead, but they are also easy to see in detail. What can we learn from nature? What can we learn from other cultures? Help the children see how we have learned to use "aspirin" from willows, we have taken steel from the rocks, and we have taken animals as symbols for our sports teams and schools, just as the indigenous people took them for totems or symbols of various values and attributes.

What is the value of these collections? Is it all right for us to use dead animals? Do we have an obligation to learn from those sacrifices we ask of other species? These are complex issues, but in reality the museum is like a bit like a mortuary. Understanding death is part of understanding life.

A word to the wise:

As adults we make assumptions that we shouldn't when visiting museums and trying to enjoy the marvelous displays. Let me give you an example from taking our grandson, Matthew, just a month short of his fourth birthday. His mom knew he loved dinosaurs and told him he was going to see lots of dinosaurs with grandpa. We went to the Field and he was anticipating this, but when we found the first dinosaur on the main floor in the large hall he looked at it and looked around and finally asked when we would see the dinosaurs. For him it was just a collection of bones. Keep that in mind as you share things that are exciting and understandable to you.

Age of grandchild: 3 and up

Best season: All

Contact: The Field Museum, 1400 South Lake Shore Drive, Chicago, IL
60605 • (312) 922-9410 • www.fieldmuseum.org

Also check out:

Illinois State Museum, Springfield; (217) 782-7386; www.museum.state.il.us

Burpee Museum of Natural History, Rockford; (815) 965-3433; www.burpee.org

Lincoln Park Zoo

This place is more than a Zoo—it is a green, peaceful oasis in the middle of a noisy metropolis. The city planners of the nineteenth century were visionaries, setting aside this plot of land, nearly on the shores of Lake Michigan as a place for the public to rejuvenate. Not only is this the oldest zoo in the country, but it is free! Today, it is a mix of the past and the future, as some of the original Georgian Revival brick buildings stand among more recent, modern structures.

A half a day is not enough time to see everything well, so you might consider limiting your choices on early visits with the younger kids, gradually extending your stays as their attention span grows. If you only want to focus on a few areas, we would recommend the following:

The Pritzker Family Children's Zoo is unique in that it focuses on four species of animals—beaver, otter, black bear and wolf. In times when the vegetation is thick, keepers will plant special treats inside small holes in the artificial tree stump and the bears will come out to investigate and try to retrieve the treats.

The beaver and otter exhibits also have an underwater viewing component that can be seen inside the Education building. But first, you must get past the plaza fountains. On a hot summer day, your grandchildren may be content to spend most of their time playing in these spurting sprays. Inside the building though, is a wonderful creation called a Climbing Tree Canopy. This multi-level play space, with netting on the sides, is limited to children under the age of 7. If you can pry them away from this part of the building, you will be able to show them exhibits with turtles, raptors, walking sticks, and the swimming otters and beavers.

Also not to be missed is the Regenstein Center for African Apes, where outdoor and indoor exhibits blend together, due to the floor to ceiling windows. At twenty nine thousand square feet, it is impressive for the visitor and a spacious home for the apes. An artificial termite mound has been built in the corner of one of the exhibits and visitors can watch as the chimps poke sticks (gathered from a pile in their exhibit) into the pre-drilled holes and pull them out with a reward of mustard, instead of the termites they would gather in the wild. Mustard! Well, these are urban chimps now.

Bonding and bridging:

The big Cat House is an interesting mix of new and old. The inside is a large echoing chamber with a high arched ceiling, and along each wall, small concrete enclosures. Instead of the bars on the cages there is a wire mesh (nearly invisible) and realistic murals in the cages as well as artificial rock work. The cats have access to large, naturalistic outdoor enclosures and this is where they spend a lot of their time.

This exhibit demonstrates how we use new knowledge to change the way we live. Look at the small exhibits and ask your grandchild how they think an animal would feel in such a space. How would the child feel confined to an area like that? Then talk about the newer outside exhibits and what they like about them. Remind them that zoos and the general public have only recently reevaluated assumptions about the health needs of captive animals.

A word to the wise:

Scattered throughout the zoo are docents—volunteers who stand at special stations with a variety of artifacts and information to share with the visitor. Some may have skulls or skins to show you, while others may be ready to tell you more about the animals in the exhibit. Most of these kinds of outdoor exhibits are in place from Memorial Day to Labor Day. After that, they may move indoors.

Age of grandchild: 2 and up

Best season: Spring or early summer, when there are likely to be more baby animals.

Contact: Lincoln Park Zoo, 2001 North Clark Street, Chicago, IL 60614 (312) 742-2000 • www.lpzoo.org

Also check out:

Brookfield Zoo, Brookfield; (708) 688-8000; www.brookfieldzoo.org

Miller Park Zoo, Bloomington; (309) 434-2509; www.millerparkzoo.org

Niabi Zoo, Coal Valley; (309) 799-3482; www.niabizoo.com

Scoville Zoo, Decatur; (217) 421-7435; www.decatur-parks.org/zoo

Life is no brief candle to me. It is a sort of splendid torch which I've got hold of for the moment and I want to make it burn as brightly as possible before handing it on to the future generations. George Bernard Shaw

John G. Shedd Aquarium

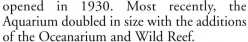

For 80 years parents and grandparents have been bringing children to this nationally known aquarium. John G. Shedd, retired president of Marshall Field & Company, in the early 1920s, decided that Chicago, to be a world-class metropolis, needed a world-class aquarium. This was the first inland aquarium with a permanent saltwater collection, which meant one million gallons of saltwater had to be shipped from Key West by train. The Aquarium opened in 1930. Most recently, the Aquarium doubled in size with the additions of the Oceanarium and Wild Reef.

Today's grandparents may very well remember their first visit to this imposing, but beautiful edifice. Its educational mission has changed, as our knowledge has grown about better ways to maintain creatures from far away oceans in human made habitats.

As you enter the main hall from the Kovler Family Hall you see the huge, circular, all glass Caribbean Reef Exhibit, filled with polychromatic fish, ancient sea turtles, and the ever popular sharks. It is a feast for the eyes and a great introduction to all the amazing animals found in the Aquarium. Another larger reef exhibit on the lower level includes more sharks, as well as the colorful coral, rays, eels, and fish. The original portion of the building holds more traditional wall-mounted tanks, with fish from around the world. One wing houses a newer exhibit called Amazon Rising, which details the human and animal dependence on the cycles of high and low water flows. The challenge in any large museum is to not become over-saturated, so that you are running past one exhibit to the next.

The most impressive and special part of the aquarium is the Oceanarium. Behind the huge dolphin tank a wall of windows faces the great lake, so that as you sit in the stands to watch the show, your eyes go out to the water beyond. You can almost imagine the dolphins have just swum in for a visit. On either side of this pool are smaller tanks holding beluga whales and sea otters. Plantings of pines and other vegetation screen the pools from one another, giving a sense of discovery as you encounter a new exhibit. The Dolphin Show is 20 minutes long, and the trainers spend time explaining different behaviors that the dolphins demonstrate. Most of these are not of the leaping variety. Many grandparents grew up watching Flipper and though fun, not everything we saw on that show was real dolphin behavior.

Bonding and bridging:

Children today know a great deal more about the oceans and their inhabitants than their grand-parents did at their age. Science and television have allowed us to see and understand so much more about these exotic creatures. The oceans, even though they exist thousands of miles away are critical to our health and survival and not just because of the food they provide. They also affect our climate and for this reason alone, we all need to care about them. Ask your grandchild to talk about ways we can all protect and enjoy our water resources, maybe as you go for a walk along the lakeside after your visit to the Shedd. If you are able—use the Shedd Aquarium visit to help plan a future trip to an ocean, where you can both don snorkels and better explore this underwater world.

A word to the wise:

The lines to get into the Shedd tend to be very long. This can be particularly uncomfortable in the summer when heat and humidity are at their worst. But there are several ways to avoid this unpleasant and inconvenient wait. You can buy a Chicago City Pass, which is good for five major attractions, including the Shedd, Adler Planetarium and the Field Museum. They are good for nine days. With one of these passes, you can enter through another door, often with no line at all. These passes can be bought at the other museums or at the Chicago Cultural Center. You may also pre-buy your tickets through Ticketmaster, online, or through a concierge service at your hotel. Finally, you can buy an annual membership to the Aquarium and this too gives you priority access, along with other special benefits.

Age of grandchild: All

Best season: Any

Contact: John G. Shedd Aquarium, 1200 South Lake Shore Drive, Chicago, IL 60605 • (312) 939-2438 • www.sheddaquarium.org

Also check out:

National Mississippi River Museum & Aquarium, Dubuque, IA; (563) 557-9545; www.rivermuseum.com

The Peggy Notebaert Nature Museum

Just next door to the Lincoln Park Zoo is a modern-looking white stone building, well screened from the roadway by lots of trees and restored prairie plantings. Built in 1999 by the Chicago Academy of Sciences, this Museum has employed some of the most up-to-date technology for "green" building, using solar panels, a green roof and lots of outdoor nature trails.

The first exhibit you come to as you enter is the Riverworks. If you have young grandchildren, you may want to divert their attention and try to get past it. This would be best saved till later in the visit, because if they are like our grandson—once he finds a water playground, it's almost impossible to pull him away. And there are many more fun things to see and do in this Center.

If you can't get past it, you will find a series of elevated tables with a variety of designs and signage that the older child or adult can read to learn about just what is being demonstrated—whether it is land use to control water usage, or a demo of the canal that runs beneath the city of Chicago and is used to prevent downpours from flooding the sewers and compromising Lake Michigan. There are locks and dams and boats that the little ones will want to play with.

Beyond this room you will pass by the Look in Animal Lab where you can peer into aquariums (both wet and dry) and see a wide assortment of insects and mammals. Interestingly, in the water filled aquariums, you can watch the water being filtered naturally below these tanks, just as it would in a real wetland.

In the Hands On Habitat you can go 'underground' in an artificially created subterranean world. The kids can stick their arms into two fabric snakes, find a mix of real and pretend animals, enjoy a slide, and climb into a tree top world. They can also walk into the make believe den of a beaver family and observe how animals use camouflage to hide.

The upper floor hosts traveling exhibits that may have an extra charge, but are exciting exhibits that keep the museum changing and challenging.

Bonding and bridging:

This Museum is all about showing connections between living organisms, including us. It is about natural and human communities and how lives in both communities are in complex webs where everything depends upon something else in order to live well.

You can show them how we can create feeders, gardens, and landscapes that support other species and allow us to live in a healthy, natural community. Let them fill your feeders and bird baths. Allow them to water plants and help you with planting.

A word to the wise:

Make sure you visit Butterfly Haven. This misty, flower-filled space is the domain of butterflies and birds. You only have to walk a few feet and find yourself surrounded by wings of all sizes, and colors. Looking closer into the vegetation you will see equally colorful birds of the tropics. The butterflies land on plants and sometimes on visitors. The only thing they ask is that you not touch the butterflies—although they are free to touch you. In the midst of an Illinois winter, this room would be an especially nice tonic.

Age of grandchild: 3 and up

Best season: Any

Contact: The Peggy Notebaert Nature Museum, 2430 North Cannon Drive, Chicago IL 60614 • (773) 755-5100 • www.naturemuseum.org

Also check out:

Burpee Museum of Natural History, Rockford; (815) 965-3433; www.burpee.org

The Science Center, Carbondale; (618) 529-5431; www.museumsusa.org/museums/info/1165321

Orpheum Children's Science Museum, Champaign; (217) 352-8160; www.m-crossroads.org/orpheum

Museum of Geology, Western Illinois University, Macomb; (309) 298-1151; www.wiu.edu/geology/museum.htm

Millennium Park

Grant Park anchors the southern end of Chicago's 23-mile-long Lake Michigan greenway allowing Chicago to boast one of the world's finest public spaces and the new Millennium Park is right up there at the top. This 24.5 acre space, the brainchild of Mayor Richard Daley, opened in 2001 replacing railroad tracks and old parking lots with a combination of daring architecture, sculpture, formal tree plantings and people-friendly promenades and plazas.

There is much to do and see at this park and the shiniest object will probably grab your attention first. It is officially called the Cloud Gate, but others call it the silver coffee bean and your grandkids may see a jelly bean. This 100 ton piece of polished stainless steel reflects all around it, including all the people

who are drawn to its curvilinear lines. This is like a funhouse mirror, distorting our bodies and the city skyline. Be sure to take photos from different angles.

After paying a visit to the "bean", you will want to stroll over to the Crown Plaza. If it is at all warm outside, plan to spend a lot of time at this spot. Two 50' glass block towers face one another, with a shallow reflecting pool between them. What makes these towers so special are the video images displayed on them—gigantic, animated faces of Chicago citizens, young and old, of all ethnic backgrounds. Watch them for a few minutes and all of a sudden you will see a mouth pucker followed by a substantial stream of water that flows out to the excited, shrill screams of the kids below. Later, water will pour over the top of the towers and down the sides, drenching all those standing purposely next to the sides of the towers. The reflecting pool really isn't a pool, since there are no sides and the water pours down through channels on either side, but there is enough water to cool everyone's feet and let the little ones splash to their heart's content.

Almost any age grandchild will enjoy getting wet at the Plaza, but older children may be more willing to move on and explore other parts of the park, like the Jay Pritzker Pavilion where free concerts are performed during the summer months. Lawns to stretch out on and tree lined promenades to stroll all create a relaxing setting for you and your grandchildren.

Bonding and bridging:

This is a park setting where kids can be kids and you can delight in their exuberance, whether it is splashing in the water at the Crown fountains, or playing catch with a Frisbee on the grass lawn in front of the Pavilion. If your grandchild is an urban dweller, they especially need the contact with green living things. A child from a rural area will be fascinated by all the people engaged in so many forms of social interaction. This is a place where people from all races and backgrounds can come and find respite from the noise and pressures of the city living. Let your grandchild be the guide in the park and lead you to the places they most want to see.

A word to the wise:

Be sure to bring along extra dry clothing when you come to this park. It's impossible for a child (and most adults) to go to the Crown Plaza and not at least wade in the water, which inevitably leads to a bit more splashing, till finally they are soaked. Be aware also that the pool surface can be slippery on bare feet and remind your grandchild not to run (a hard thing to resist). The water runs (weather permitting) from mid-April to mid-October. Come back in the winter and the water has changed to ice, although not at the Crown Plaza, but nearby at the McCormick Tribune Plaza and Ice Rink.

Age of grandchild: 2 and up

Best season: Summer

Contact: Millennium Park; Michigan Avenue to the west, Columbus Drive to the east, Randolph Street to the North and Monroe Street to the South (312) 742-1168 • www.millenniumpark.org

Also check out:

Buckingham Fountain, Chicago;
www.chicagoparkdistrict.com/index.cfm/fuseaction/buckinghamfountain.fo
untainhome

Gateway Geyser Fountain, East St. Louis;
http://lewisandclarktrail.com/section1/illinoiscities/gatewaygeyser.htm

Museum of Science and Industry

The best Chicago museum might not be found on the "Museum Campus" or along the famous Grant Park lakefront. It is not on the magnificent mile or tucked into one of the bustling streets. This museum is in a quiet location close to the shore and it takes some work to get here since the trolleys and El do not serve it, but do not let the location, the name and the imposing building put you off. It will be no surprise if you and your grandchildren are not soon caught up in discovery and play and wishing you had more time.

Imagine walking in to find a full Pioneer Zephyr train sitting within the building! And if that doesn't get your curiosity going, try the submarine or airplanes hanging from the ceiling.

These are not just static exhibits. This is a building of innovation and exploration. The full-size train is complimented by a 3,500 square foot layout called the "Great Train Story" that is the dream of model railroaders. Get down to your grandchild's level and journey with the train as it crosses a miniature America. Grandchildren will run from place to place, find favorite sites and observe the combination of natural landscapes, cities, and industries shipping apples, lumber and other raw materials, blow the whistles and horns, move containers and otherwise get engaged.

Go onboard the submarine, watch video stories, touch and explore artifacts from this dramatic part of World War II when Germany's undersea capacity for terror threatened to take the ocean away from the Western powers. The story of the seas is complicated and well developed with both the actual submarine and the creative story-telling that surrounds it. If they enjoy space they can look at the Apollo 8 Command Module, the Lunar Module, Mercury Space Capsule, and the Henry Crown Space Center.

Less dramatic, but completely captivating for the children is an exhibit that allows them to watch toys being made! Now THIS is something they can relate to. Small children can also relate to Colleen Moore's Fairy Castle, the Chick Hatchery, Robots Like Us, and Yesterday's Main Street.

Bonding and bridging:

Be sure to visit the Idea Factory. This is a children's museum within a museum, part of the museum's imagination station. You can help them grasp the simple basics that have led to our amazing scientific achievements. For example, a cube, sphere, tetrahedron and cylinder are all that are required for the children to learn about ideas as diverse as construction, magnetism, and air and water!

Always popular, water is given a special place in the learning setting. Hand/eye coordination is developed as they build and navigate their own little boats or work the electromagnetic crane.

We worry about the lack of scientific knowledge in our children, but here is the perfect place for the grandparent to encourage their activity and ask, "How did that happen?"

A word to the wise:

Reusable City brings science to the home and the neighborhood. Explore pollution, learn about monitoring. See how one action can lead to unexpected results. If your grandchildren are caught up in the ideas from the popular CSI series that uses science to uncover clues, they will love this laboratory and the ability to test, explore, and make some decisions about where and how they live.

Age of grandchild: 5 and up

Best season: All

Contact: Museum of Science and Industry, 57th Street and Lake Shore Drive, Chicago, IL 60637 • (773) 684-1414 • www.msichicago.org

Also check out:

SciTech Hands On Museum, Aurora; (630) 859-3434; http://scitech.mus.il.us

Orpheum Children's Science Museum, Champaign; (217) 352-5895; www.m-crossroads.org/orpheum

The Peggy Notebaert Nature Museum, Chicago; (773) 755-5100; www.chias.org

Just when I thought I was too old to fall in love again, I became a Grandparent. UNKNOWN

Touch the Sky

Humans have always seemed to envy birds and tried to emulate them, and in recent history we have developed ways to put our buildings into the clouds. Chicago has a skyline made up of "skyscrapers." The word came into popular usage in the 1880s, when steel skeleton framing allowed the construction of tall, multistory buildings over 500 feet tall.

Chicago is considered by many as the birthplace of the skyscraper—the 10 story Home Insurance Building. However, its leading position was lost because of height limitations set by building codes. When those were relaxed in 1960, the city rushed ahead to regain its place of prominence in the world

of skyscrapers. In 1969, the John Hancock Building opened with 100 floors. Soon to follow were the Aon Center (originally the Standard Oil Building) in 1973, with 83 floors. New York's Empire State Building was the tallest in the world from 1931 until 1973 when the Sears Tower in Chicago opened with 105 floors and a 278' antenna.

Both the Hancock and the Sears Tower have viewing areas open to the public. In the Hancock, you can ride the elevators up to the 94th floor. In the open air walkway you can really appreciate the title "windy city" and enjoy exhibits along the walls that detail the history of the city. Interactive computers and Soundscopes (a telescope with sound effects) allow you to see even further and hear the city. For a real memento, have your grandchild pose in front of one of the scenes that show them relaxing on a beam high above the earth or washing the windows of the building.

The Sears Tower also has an observatory called the Skydeck, at 1353 feet, even higher than the John Hancock's. Everyone will feel their ears popping as they ride the elevators at 1600 feet per minute. This observation area also has historical exhibits, telescopes and computers to enhance the experience. Show your grandchild the lower level display that allows them to see the history and other facts about the city through kid size cut-out windows.

Then gaze off into the distance; look below at the miniature cars and city life, peek into three states, share a sense of adventure and maybe stomach butterflies. If you're lucky (as we were), you might catch sight of a falcon soaring effortlessly at eye level in search of its next meal.

Bonding and bridging:

Skyscrapers are just a fact of life for our grandchildren, but even so there is a natural sense of awe standing at the base of one of these monumental structures as you tilt your neck back as far as it will go to see the top. It can make a person feel very small and in that sense you can relate to your grandchild's perspective of the world in the early years of their lives. For a while, everything looks gigantic to them. It can also provide you with an immense respect for the technical and physical skills needed to build such an edifice. Play with numbers before or after your visit (get the calculator out if you need to) and have your grandchild multiply their height the necessary number of times to find out how many of them, standing on top of each other, it would take to reach the top.

A word to the wise:

If you would like to make a visit to one of these skyscrapers extra special, arrange to have a meal at the Signature Restaurant on the 95th floor of the John Hancock Building. Here you will have a window seat (floor to ceiling) on the world. You will have plenty of time to look out at the lake and discuss what you see, as you wait for your food to arrive and while you eat. Plan the event for the evening and you will have a magical setting as you look out over the city of lights spanning all directions. While this is a wonderful place to eat, keep in mind that for the children it is a place of awe and the meal might be a distant second for their attention.

Age of grandchild: 3 and up

Best season: Any

Contact:

John Hancock Observatory, 875 North Michigan Avenue, Chicago, IL 60661 • (888) 875-8439 • www.hancockobservatory.com

Sears Tower, 233 South Wacker Drive, Suite 3530, Chicago, IL 60606 (312) 875-9447• www.theskydeck.com

Also check out:

Illinois State Capitol; www.online-springfield.com/sites/capitol.html

Perfect love sometimes does not come until grandchildren are born. WELSH PROVERB

Wrigley Field

With all due respect to the southsiders (the White Sox for any possible non-baseball fans), Wrigley Field is one of the wonders of the sports world, a Mecca that few venues can match. Lambeau Field, Fenway Park, the Boston Gardens —the list is short although many people can argue for their favorite places and some might even argue for Soldier Field, but in the world of sports there are only a limited number of places where the location is as much of a draw as the team that plays in it. And considering the record of the Cubbies over the years—it might not be a stretch to say that this park far outdraws its tenants.

Built in 1914 for less than the annual salary of the lowest player on the current team, this stadium has managed to be part of all the primary eras of baseball history, and grandchildren who are captivated by the players, the numbers, and the majesty of the sport will know that this was the place where legends played—Banks, Wilson, Jenkins, Sandberg and others who are in the Hall of Fame, or in the pantheon of baseball lore.

The stadium is not only old, but is part of the neighborhood. It is the focal point for the north side and the loveable losers that are the Cubs baseball team will always hold out hope, but will remain popular even if they continue to disappoint and never win.

Entering this stadium with its real grass and bleachers that look like bleachers, provides the atmosphere that captivates both generations. The ivy covered walls are classic, the home runs landing on the street, or the long fly balls being blown back into the stadium by Lake Michigan winds provide great stories.

Stadium food is still a strong tradition and the smells of hotdogs and popcorn are sensual parts of the experience, along with the crunch of peanut shells underfoot, and barking of the vendors.

Singing "Take Me Out to the Ball Game" at the seventh inning stretch reaches its zenith in this park and you and your grandchildren will have as much fun singing, listening, eating, and watching the spectators, as you do watching the ball game. No wonder it does not take a winner to attract a big crowd.

Bonding and bridging:

Mike's childhood was affected by some strong influences, but none more than his great uncle Clarence who would share the sports page while watching one game on television and listening to another on radio. A vet who was severely wounded in WWI, Clarence found his outlet as a fan and imparted this love through stories about the past, statistics, and images of baseball as he knew it. This imparted a lifetime passion for the sport to Mike and also was an example of bridging and bonding through stories. Mike's grandfather (Clarence's brother) would play catch and show him how to throw the ball. But the game of catch was always a combination of imagination and exercise.

A word to the wise:

If there is a better example of the importance of how you play the game being more important than winning, we do not know where it would be. The most beloved of all Cubs—Ernie Banks—was famous for his smile and demeanor, as much as for his 500 home runs. "Let's play two," was his rallying cry, but poor Ernie never really played on a winner. He had famous teammates make the Hall of Fame with him, but they could not find a way to make the World Series. Yet people kept coming out. In an era where winning seems to be everything, this could be one of the most important lessons you can teach. Baseball is still a game and games should be fun, should be filled with sportsmanship, and each person who plays should do so with pride regardless of the outcome.

Age of grandchild: 7 and up

Best season: Summer

Contact: Wrigley Field, 1060 West Addison Street, Chicago, IL 60613
(773) 404-CUBS• http://chicago.cubs.mlb.com
www.ballparks.com/baseball/national/wrigle.htm

Also check out:

Soldier Field—Bears football, Chicago; (312) 235-7000;
www.soldierfield.net

Chicago Botanic Garden

World-class is the only way to describe the Chicago Botanic Garden. Opened in 1972, the 385 acres include three natural areas and 23 distinct formal garden displays. Every season of the year provides an entirely different palette of colors, shapes, and textures in the 2.3 million plants that make up this vast living collection.

It is no wonder that each year nearly 800,000 visitors come to this treasure located just north of metropolitan Chicago. But there is one particular garden you and your grandchild will probably want to visit first and frequently—the

Landmarks of America Model Railroad Garden. While admission to the main Botanic Garden is free, there is a small fee for admission to this magical land of miniature and it is well worth the investment to see the eyes light up and smiles spread as your grandchild encounters this hidden world of model trains and landscapes. There are 15 trains, all running at the same time over trestles, through bridges and past tiny towns and miniaturized American monuments (Mt. Rushmore, Wrigley Field, the Statue of Liberty, etc).

While the kids crouch down to watch the trains chug past, you can sit on a bench and take in the whole nostalgic scene, as well as marvel at the detail and incredible imagination and labor required to create this garden. All the buildings and bridges are made from pieces of nature—the trestle bridges from twigs; the roof shingles from overlapping leaves, lamp posts with acorns topping the poles. It really is astounding and it is all the creation of Paul Busse.

Yes, the Model Train Garden will delight you and your grandchild for years. It is only open from the middle of May until the end of October, but you don't have to wait six and a half months to enjoy this treat from the past. From late October to early January the train moves indoors and becomes the Wonderland Express.

When you can finally pry the children away from the Train Garden, lead them on a journey to one of the other fascinating and beautiful spots in this shrine to Mother Nature.

Bonding and bridging:

If possible, begin taking your grandchild to the Chicago Botanic Garden when they are still in strollers. To toddlers, every living thing is fascinating and they are ready to be thrilled by the smells and textures of the Garden. A garden is a place of quiet, and "take time to smell the roses" is a lesson desperately needed in today's world. Here you can help your grandchild to focus on the incredible mystery of flowers—their delicate scents and fragile petals. Walk through the prairie, with its billowing grasses and longer view, and feel the freedom of the open spaces.

A word to the wise:

Because this is such a large, spread out Botanic Garden, don't try to do or see too much in one visit. You want your grandchild to want to return so save certain parts of the garden for later visits. Be sure everyone wears comfortable walking shoes, because there are miles of foot paths that meander from one garden to the next and lots of benches. If walking distances is difficult for either adult or child, there are two different 35 minute tram tours that run from the end of April to the end of October. Be sure to check at the Visitor Center when you arrive for special, free activity cards that the kids can use to help them find specific plants and animals as you walk around. This is a souvenir you can date and save for them.

Age of grandchild: All

Best season: All

Contact: Chicago Botanic Garden, 1000 Lake Cook Road, Glencoe, IL 60022 • (847) 835-5440 • www.chicagobotanic.org

Also check out:

Garfield Park Conservatory, Chicago; (312) 746-5100; www.garfield-conservatory.org

Klehm Arboretum, Rockford; (815) 965-8146; www.klehm.org

Morton Arboretum, Lisle; (630) 968-0074; www.mortonarb.org

Washington Park Botanical Garden, Springfield; (217) 544-1751; www.springfieldparks.org/garden

Spring Valley Nature Sanctuary & Volkening Heritage Farm

Want to get out of the city, but not have to go too far? Want to explore the natural landscape of the prairie without making your grandchild spend too much time in the car? Want to find a collection of historic farm buildings, trails that can give you good exercise, bird watching and wildflowers, where the buildings are the best of green architecture? If so, Spring Valley Nature Center, located in Schaumberg, in the northwest part of the metropolitan area of Chicago, is one of the best in the state.

The Center is designed to accommodate groups—schools, scouts, clubs—but don't let that keep you from walking and searching the grounds and the building. It is open to the public and you are welcomed in many ways. There are places to sit and explore inside the building and there are hikes and programs by professional educators that will enthrall you and your grandchildren. Sometimes the pleasure of seeing your grandchildren learn makes you more open to learning.

There are five primary trails from the Nature Center—the shortest is .5 miles to the Merkle Cabin, open on Sunday afternoons so you can participate in an activity, or sit by the fireplace, and relax. Next is the .7 mile trail to the Heritage Farm, a recreation of an historic German farm with interpreters in costume and the opportunity to participate in some of the farm chores. This trail to the farm is called the Footprints on the Land Trail and helps connect you to the history of people and the land, a great transition between the two building sites. The Bob Link Arboretum is just a .75 mile walk and the Illinois Habitat trail explores wetlands, woodlands, and prairie on a 1.2 mile walk.

Driving by the park your first impression might be that they forgot to mow the grass. But that is because we are so used to our manicured landscape and when nature displays some wildness it demands more than a glance to see the subtle beauty and diversity. The value of a place just a few miles from millions of people is that you can get to it often, listen to the changes in sound, observe the shifts in color, and even experience the variety of weather that is impossible when we stay inside.

Bonding and bridging:

The combination of nature center and historic farm places a wonderful emphasis on the mixing of human and natural systems and gives you a chance to discuss how people and nature interact. Why do some people have a lot of birds in their yard and others have none? What is the value of parks that are nature oriented or those for active play? We can never get away from nature. We need it for breathing, drinking, growing food, constructing our communities, but what does nature need us for? Being a good steward of the land should be something we all strive for.

A word to the wise:

There are four family events that are perfect opportunities for all of you. Check out the Sugar Bush in March when the maple trees are tapped and syrup is made. Then come to the Backyards for Nature plant sale—bring home some native plants for your home. Let the grandchild water and care for them. In June there is a Picnic in the Pasture with music, hayrides and barbeques, and finally in October is the Harvest Festival at the farm and cabin with more music, hayrides and the taste of the harvest.

Age of grandchild: All

Best season: Spring when birds, bugs and woodland blooms are out and summer when the prairie is in flower

Contact: Schaumburg Park District, 1111 E. Schaumburg Road Schaumburg, IL 60194 • (847) 985-2100 • http://www.parkfun.com

Also check out:

North Park Village Nature Center, Chicago; (312) 744-5472; www.chicagoparkdistrict.com/index.cfm

Red Oak Nature Center; Batavia; (630) 897-1808; www.foxvalleyparkdistrict.org

Walter Heller Nature Center, Highland Park; (847) 831-3810; www.pdhp.org/index.cfm

Peggy Notebaert Nature Museum, Chicago; (773) 755-5100; www.chias.org

Grandchildren are God's way of compensating us for growing old. MARY H. WALDRIP

Ravinia Festival

It's all right to step up and let your grandchildren experience something that seems very adult. As a matter of fact it is essential that you help break some of the artificial barriers children seem to acquire through peer pressure. Think of how much fun young children have dressing up and pretending to be adults. Now think about dressing nice, going to a fancy location, having a picnic in the grass and listening to classical music—it doesn't get much better than that.

In 1904 this site began as an amusement park. Now, over 100 years old, the Ravinia Music Festival is the continent's oldest outdoor music event. Ravinia calls itself an experience. Enter the gates and find the perfect picnic spot on the lawn and settle in. Of course, making this special means making your picnic special too. A few extra items you might not normally include with a picnic are worth splurging on here—like sparkling fruit juice that looks so adult, but is great for the kids. Then, during intermission, you can treat everyone to an ice cream cone.

From your picnic spot you can watch the stars shine in the sky and listen to the stars perform on stage. The 3,200 seat Pavilion is an open air venue for the Chicago Symphony Orchestra and serves as a performance stage for top acts in jazz, pop, folk, blues, and country music.

The Martin Theater is steps away from the train and is the only original building that dates back to the park's opening in 1904. This is an 850 seat "recital hall" where jazz is performed, as well as chamber music and vocal performances. Like the Pavilion, each performance is broadcast onto the lawn.

This lawn is expansive and well groomed. There are picnic tables and blanket spaces, as well as the best outdoor sound system around. A good time to test this activity on young grandchildren is Saturday mornings when they have a series of 11 a.m. concerts and programs geared to the children.

There is also a special series to introduce the kids to classical music. These special dates are called Family Space and in addition to picnic and music they have an 'instrument petting zoo' where the children can try them out, plus other arts and crafts related to the music.

Bonding and bridging:

Music is one of the great means of communication in the world. We listen to birds and hear music, we record the sounds of whales and other mammals who communicate in patterns and sound waves. Human cultures have integrated music into religion, relaxation, and entertainment. Many people put their children to bed with the sounds of waves or soft music to sooth them.

What is it about music that so appeals to us. What songs do you remember from high school or college? What are the special songs between the grandparents? Can you talk about music and find special pieces that will unite you with your grandchildren? Think of how wonderful it would be to hear a song and remember your time together.

A word to the wise:

If you find the idea of planning and packing the picnic too laborious, don't worry, the food kiosks at Ravinia are not the run-of-the-mill variety. If you want this to be elegant, you can ignore their salads and burgers and go for the gourmet sandwiches and wood-fired pizzas. You can also get gourmet cheeses and spreads, fresh fruit and veggies, ice cream and desserts, coffee, soft drinks, wine, beer and cocktails. You should also check their website to see what is prohibited. They do not allow things that would detract from the general atmosphere even though you might take them on another picnic.

Age of grandchild: All

Best season: Summer

Contact: Ravinia Festival, 418 Sheridan Road, Highland Park, IL 60035
(847) 266-5100 • http://www.ravinia.org

Also check out:

Summerwood outdoor concerts, Rockford; (800) 521-0849; www.gorockford.com/calendar.asp

Cantigny Park Sunday Outdoor Concert Series, Wheaton; (630) 668-5161; www.mccormicktribune.org/museumsparks/cantignypark.aspx

Rock Island outdoor concerts and plays; (309) 732-2000; www.rigov.org/citydepartments/parks/parkinfo.html

I've learned that when your newly born grandchild holds your little finger in his fist, that you're hooked for life. ANDY ROONEY

Volo Bog State Natural Area

If you can't make a trip to the North Country, perhaps you should visit a portion of the north country that came to Illinois. In northeast Illinois, just south of the Wisconsin border, but only a half hour from the large metropolitan areas along Lake Michigan, is Volo Bog.

If you are unfamiliar with the term bog, it refers to a unique wetland that is found throughout Canada and the northern fringe of states, but not the middle

or southern states. The water is acidic, the soil is really a plant (sphagnum), and the trees bounce on the far side of the wetland when someone steps on the sphagnum mat. The plants that grow here have strange names like sundew and pitcher plant, and some species are even carnivorous and eat insects. Tamaracks are members of the pine family that lose their needles, and the entire area is a dream landscape unlike anything else in Illinois.

Talk about exotic travel on a budget! This gift of the continental glaciers was documented in 1921 and protected by the Nature Conservancy, then the University of Illinois, and finally the Department of Natural Resources. Now it is open to everyone and has well-designed exhibits and displays to help you understand this unique place inside the wonderful renovated dairy barn visitor center.

At one time this was a fifty foot deep lake, but that changed over a 6,000 year history. Two trails help you explore: the 2.75 mile Tamarack Trail rings the bog, enters forests and fields, prairies, and wetlands, giving a view of glacial features, a prairie restoration, and a savannah as well as the bog and all its plants and animals. The observation blind is a good place to sit, have a snack, and wait for wildlife—birds and beaver come in to view. The best luck will come in early morning or evening.

The real treat for the kids and you (but watch out if you have balance problems) is the main interpretive trail. Here is a floating board walk that dips and bounces with each step. It takes you into the wetlands and lets you see up close the water dock, cinnamon fern, royal fern, arrowhead, pitcher plants, orchids and tamarack trees. Talk about beauty and diversity!

Remember that you will see more uniqueness than your grandchild, because you have more to compare things to. This is just one more memory and snapshot of the world for your grandchild's growing knowledge and it will be more important with each new experience.

Bonding and bridging:

Talk about where you live. What makes it a community? Does it have a boundary—a limit? Are there more communities outside of the one you live in? Does your city have a downtown area? Are there rings of suburbs? Are there outlying rural areas?

Take those ideas and look at the microcosm that is Volo Bog. From the eye to the shoreline we see rings of development, each ring structure slightly different from the others that border it, just like our urban communities. We can tell where our bog ends, but then what? There is a hickory forest, over there is grassland—each landscape different, each unique, each a community in nature.

A word to the wise:

Bring a picnic and spend the day. The bog offers wonderful programs for the general public (they do require reservations) and these can be shared experiences. Some programs, like the aqua safari, are very hands-on and they invite children as young as 5 to participate. Most Saturdays and Sundays there are guided tours and often bird hikes. Get their information and check out a program that you can all enjoy. It is nice when you can be on equal terms with your grandchild.

Age of grandchild: 5 and up

Best season: Spring, summer and fall

Contact: Volo Bog State Natural Area, 28478 West Brandenburg Road, Ingleside, IL 60041 • (815) 344-1294
http://dnr.state.il.us/lands/landmgt/parks/r2/volobog.htm

Also check out:

Cache River State Natural Area, Shawnee Forest; (618) 634-9678; http://dnr.state.il.us/lands/landmgt/parks/r5/cachervr.htm

Bell Smith Springs, Shawnee Forest; (618) 658-2111; www.visitusa.com/illinois/hiking/bellsmithspringstrailsystem.htm

Franklin Creek State Natural Area, Franklin Grove; (815) 456-2878; http://dnr.state.il.us/lands/landmgt/parks/r1/franklin.htm

Goose Lake Prairie State Natural Area, Morris; (815) 942-2899; http://dnr.state.il.us/lands/landmgt/parks/l&m/east/goose/home.htm

Illinois Railway Museum

Do you remember when we were young, and trains were among the most exciting things in the world, hearing that horn blast in the distance? A train rolling through our neighborhood was a special event. We all gathered and waved, hoping the man in the caboose would wave back. The Illinois Railway Museum has captured some of that magic, allowing us to share it with our grandchildren.

The Museum is located just outside the town of Union, a small town with a wonderful name, but hardly one we have had on our travel itinerary. In the northeastern part of the state, west of Marengo, it is a perfect place. This allows the visitor to concentrate on the rural depot, the tracks, and the trains and visit the nearby model railroad museum.

Arriving at the depot you are immediately impressed by the multiple tracks and the variety of engines and working cars. These trains have been given loving attention and now shine in the sun for you to inspect as though they were in their prime. In addition, the site has 9 barns, all filled with a variety of railroad paraphernalia. Choose the barns that relate to you and your grandchild. One barn has wooden rapid transit cars, another has street cars and "L" cars.

If your grandchildren have enjoyed Thomas the Train, they will enjoy the big steam locomotive barn where the massive engines have names like Sante Fe 2903, Old Smokey, and Little Joe.

You will want to ride around the yard on the street car and take a 10 mile round trip passage to Kishwaukee Grove on an electric Interurban Train pulled behind one of the large steam engines, or take the ride on a 1950s diesel passenger train. The sound of the wheels on the track, the steam, the whistle, the movement that is only found on railroads, makes for a day filled with memories.

Bonding and bridging:

It's hard for children to realize how important the railroad was in opening the West. Towns survived if the railroad came through and collapsed if it didn't. Today we worry about where roads, freeways, and airports will go.

These railroads were the clocks of the land. There were no computers or satellites to give the right time. But the railroads tried to be on time. The conductor's clock traveled with him and, along with the news, he brought the time to each community. Can your grandchildren imagine how independent and isolated we were before the Internet and cell phones? You might want to ask them if it is a good thing that we have lost that sense of separateness.

A word to the wise:

The drive to and from places like the museum can either be long and boring or add to the experience. Try to look at the variety of vehicles on the road, on the farms, along your route. What are the different roles each plays in our life and our history? And don't forget to observe the horses, cattle and dogs. Both horses and oxen pulled carts, and dogs pulled the travois. Ask them how they will travel fifty years from now.

Age of grandchild: All

Best season: Summer

Contact: Illinois Railway Museum, 7000 Olson Road, Union, IL 60180 (800) BIG-RAIL • www.irm.org

Also check out:

Fox River Trolley Museum, South Elgin; (847) 697-4676; www.foxtrolley.org

Monticello Railway Museum, Monticello; (217) 762-9011; www.mrym.org

Galesburg Railroad Museum, Galesburg; (309) 342-9400; www.galesburgrailroadmuseum.org

Fever River Railroad Museum, Freeport; (815) 233-4410

At age seven, children have as passionate a longing for creative interactions and learning as they earlier had for explorations of the world. JOSEPH CHILTON PEARCE, *THE MAGICAL CHILD*

Discovery Center Museum & Burpee Museum of Natural History

It might seem like a visit to one Children's Museum is the same as the next, but when a museum is ranked in the top ten in the nation, there is a reason for a special trip.

Creative play is the tool in the success of this experience. Grandparents need to suspend reality and engage in the mind of the grandchild. Don't worry if they get wet in the water areas—bring extra clothing.

Do not try to do everything; it is more important to get fully engaged and the Discovery Center Museum has over 250 exciting hands-on exhibits on two floors and outside in the Museum's backyard.

The building also includes the Burpee Museum of Natural History, which offers dramatic views of the state and both its current and ancient natural his-

tory. They also host traveling exhibits, special events and programs throughout the year. It is good to blend the activities in the Children's Museum and the investigations in the Natural History Museum.

Inside you can explore air and flight, learn how amusement park rides work, work with magnets and electricity, investigate weather (you can create a tornado), do math puzzles, explore color and light, find out about simple machines that are the basis for physics, discover robotics, explore construction with the indoor crane, and pretend to be the newscaster in the TV studio.

The Science Park is the largest volunteer-built exhibit of its kind. Walk wooden catwalks, archaeological digs, and complex and wet water works. Bring a change of clothes! Throughout this playground maze of bridges and turns, there are lessons in energy and physics, plus the added benefit of being outside. Fresh air, bird songs, and the Rockford River make this a great place to play.

The Museum understands the role of the grandparent and encourages them to participate. If you live in the area and can return regularly, they offer the Grand Pass which covers two grandparents and all of their grandchildren under the age of 18.

Bonding and bridging:

In your lifetime science has changed the world in almost unimaginable ways. We've gone from space exploration to the computer and the Internet that keep you connected to your family and the world. Sometimes we forget to honor the science and the scientists who paved the way for these inventions and changes. Throughout both of these wonderful museums we can be awed by the pulleys and chains, or the Ordovician sea that once covered the area, but the really important lesson is how important and exciting science is. Perhaps there is a discovery waiting for your grandchildren to find! So play, encourage testing and observations and help them to put science into their life.

A word to the wise:

The two museums are connected by an indoor walkway and they complement one another. The centerpiece of the Natural History Museum is the dinosaur named Jane. It is a dramatic presentation, complemented by wonderful graphics and lighting. But don't stop there, the third floor is a Children's Discovery Center where you can add hands-on science to your grandchild's experience and you can spend time watching paleontology and biology experts work with specimens in the Dean Olson Specimen viewing lab.

Age of grandchild:

Discovery Center: 2 to 12
Burpee Museum: 2 and up

Best season: All

Contact:

Discovery Center Museum, 711 North Main Street, Rockford, IL 61103 (815) 963-6769 • www.discoverycentermuseum.org

Burpee Museum of Natural History, 737 North Main Street, Rockford, IL 61103 • (815) 965-3433 • www.burpee.org

The simplest toy, one which even the youngest child can operate, is called a grandparent. SAM LEVENSON

Anderson Japanese Gardens

A traditional Japanese garden has as its purpose to create a setting that evokes peace and tranquility—not to display a wide variety of flowering plants. You will always find three essential elements in a Japanese garden. They are water, rocks, and plants in a variety of textures and shapes. In every part of the garden you will hear the sound of water – splashing, dripping, or flowing. It contains reflections of the sky and trees and creates a great sense of ease. While there is a diversity of plants, the overall sense is simplicity.

The Anderson Japanese Gardens began in 1978, when John and Linda Anderson commissioned a Japanese landscape designer to create this serene retreat within the limits of busy Rockford. Cars rush by on the highways next to the Garden, but once you walk through the Southern Garden Gate, the noise fades away and with it the frazzled feelings that can come from everyday lives.

This Garden should be shared with the grandchild who is old enough to understand that it is a place of quiet contemplation. This is not a park for running and yelling, but a place that has lots of hidden nooks and crannies to be discovered by the curious and respectful visitors.

As you meander down the gravel paths, you will cross six bridges. Each bridge presents you with another setting, but children especially seem to enjoy peering over the railings or sides of the bridges into the water below. The Zig Zag Bridge is based on Japanese folklore that says evil spirits only travel in straight lines. When you think about it, many cultures have stories about bridges and monsters, or other unsavory characters. Maybe your grandchild has heard the story of Billy Goat Gruff or the Norwegian trolls who hide under bridges.

While flowers are not a key component of this garden, each season has its own beautiful colors. In springtime there are flowering shrubs and trees; in the summer irises bloom near the streams and water lilies float on the ponds; autumn has the bright maple leaves.

Bonding and bridging:

This is a place to walk hand in hand with your grandchild, speaking softly and just slowly moving through the parts of the garden. Stop regularly. Ask your grandchildren what they hear. Chances are good that it will be the sound of falling water and maybe some birds singing. Ask your grandchildren how this garden makes them feel. Bring along sketch pads and watercolors, colored pencils, or pastels. Or bring along a book of Haiku poems to read aloud and then take turns writing some of your own. The pattern is three lines: the first has 5 syllables, the 2nd has 7 syllables and the 3rd has 5 again. Write one of them in the back of this book in the notes section. The lesson you want to share is the pleasure of taking a break, of contemplation and quiet.

A word to the wise:

There are more rules in this garden then others you may have visited, but they are not unreasonable. No food or beverages are allowed, people are asked to stay on the paths, and at the viewing house and tea house you should only use your eyes to appreciate the design and fine craftsmanship of these handmade structures. At the tea house, a moss garden and water basins are also just 'look—don't touch.' Volunteer docents throughout the garden will happily answer questions and guide you to other stops.

Age of grandchild: 4 and up

Best season: Spring, summer and fall (open May 1–October 31)

Contact: Anderson Japanese Gardens, 318 Spring Creek Road, Rockford, IL 61107 • (815) 229-9390 • www.andersongardens.org

Also check out:

Morton Arboretum, Lisle; (630) 719-7956; www.mortonarb.org

Chicago Botanic Garden, Glencoe; (847) 835-5440; www.chicago-botanic.org

Anna Bethel Fisher Rock Garden, Decatur; (217) 422-5911; www.decatur-parks.org/main/parks_gardens.htm

Osaka Garden, Chicago; www.hydepark.org/parks/osaka2.htm

They say genes skip generations. Maybe that's why grandparents find their grandchildren so likeable. Joan McIntosh

55

Brookfield Zoo

People have been watching animals from the beginning of time. At first, it was part of survival. We became a top predator on the food chain and much of what we learned about hunting, we learned by observing other predators. Time passed and we humans tired of the hunter-gatherer lifestyle and we became farmers. We learned how to domesticate some of the wild animals in order to harness their strength to help us work and to make the acquisition of our food less dangerous and uncertain.

After human culture developed cities, writing and the first empires, we begin to see the first zoos in the Near East and Egypt. These were strictly for the

entertainment and curiosity of the ruling classes. Later, the first zoo in China was founded by the Emperor Wen Wang. The Greeks and Romans also kept private zoos. In 1907, a German animal dealer and zoo owner by the name of Carl Hagenbac developed a new way of exhibiting animals—using a moat. This style spread around the world and is today in almost all zoos. It dramatically improved the life of zoo animals and the experience for visitors.

In the last half of the twentieth century, the concept of zoos as strictly entertainment facilities was replaced with an understanding that the animals could educate as well as entertain us and that we may be responsible for them with the loss of habitat around the world. So were born conservation and breeding programs in zoos.

We have not lost our fascination with animals, and children seem to be especially enraptured by all things that creep, crawl, fly and swim. At 14 months, our grandson, Ryan, who could barely see over the concrete wall, was captivated by the sight of giraffes; we could barely peel him away from this exhibit.

Of the many zoos in Illinois, the two most famous are Brookfield and Lincoln Park, both within the borders of Chicago. Of the 25 most popular zoos in the U.S., the Lincoln Park ranks #8, with 3 million visitors per year, and the Brookfield is #11 with 2.2 million visitors.

Bonding and bridging:

The excitement of a child seeing new, living creatures is contagious and you will find yourself remembering the thrill you felt the first time you saw a lion or a giraffe. We are all fascinated by animals, especially those we may never see in the wild. Some animals are known to be dangerous to humans, but we can watch from a safe distance and marvel at their grace and beauty. 'Funny,' 'scary,' 'amazing' all describe the sights in a zoo. The zoo gives us a chance to talk about the animals that live in the wild. Why are some endangered? And what can we do to help them? You may talk with an older child about the questions of captivity: Is it right, and if so, why? Kids really do empathize with animals. They want to be good caretakers and we grandparents should nurture that empathy.

A word to the wise:

The Primate Building at the Brookfield Zoo, while it looks something like a concrete aircraft hangar, allows you to observe the gorillas in their family units. Various ages of gorillas interact with one another and it is sometimes unnerving to recognize behavior so similar to our own. Primates are in jeopardy due to habitat loss and expanding human populations. As stewards of the planet, it is our responsibility to care about their fate. A larger than life postcard at the exit is addressed to All Human Primates and says—"Help! I'm in trouble. I Need You. I know you can help me. The Earth."

Age of grandchild: All

Best season: Any

Contact: Brookfield Zoo, 3300 Golf Road, Brookfield, IL 60513
(708) 688-8000 • www.brookfieldzoo.org

Also check out:

Lincoln Park Zoo, Chicago; (312) 742-2000; www.lpzoo.com

Miller Park Zoo, Bloomington; (309) 434-2250; www.millerparkzoo.org

Niabi Zoo, Coal Valley; (309) 799-3482; www.niabizoo.com

Midewin National Tallgrass Prairie & Goose Lake Prairie State Natural Area

In the lore of America is the image of wagon trains moving through grass so tall that kids, pets, and sometimes cattle and horses disappeared from sight. It's hard to imagine in the short grass hayfields and mowed lawns that surround our homes and settlements, but there is a place to test that image and celebrate the diversity and beauty of the natural grasslands that preceded the wagons and plows. Midewin National Tallgrass Prairie is converting a military arsenal and old farm lands into a 31,000 acre prairie landscape. Goose Lake Prairie State Natural

Area is nearby and already an established high quality prairie, and the two of them are complemented by the nearby Des Plaines Conservation Area and Heidecke Fish and Wildlife Area.

The Forest Service administers the grassland and operates a visitor center that helps put human and natural history in perspective. This is the place to begin your exploration. There are tours of grassland birds, bike rides, horseback guided rides, and archaeological sites that tell of the indigenous people's history. Tours also help tell the story of the ammunition plant that preceded the Refuge. The twilight bike rides, bunkers walk and cemetery tours have a nice spooky feeling for your grandchildren to exercise their imagination. The full moon campfire brings in storytellers and a native (midewin) speaker presents programs for kids.

Goose Lake Prairie State Natural Area begins at a visitor center with excellent displays and a roof top observation deck that allows you to peek into three counties. This "sea of grass with pretty flowers" that greeted the Illinois pioneers was sculpted by glaciers and destroyed by the plow, soon changing the Illinois "prairie state" into a cultivated field state. By 1969 the 14,000 year old prairies had nearly disappeared and the Goose Lake site was the largest remnant left. Now the original 240 acres has grown to 2,537 and the ancient grassland has been preserved.

There are miles of trails to explore and trail maps are available at the visitor center. At Goose Lake Prairie, the 20' x 20' restored cabin of John and Agnes Cragg, with a loft, was called "the palace." See if your grandchildren agree with the name.

Bonding and bridging:

We are used to having all the things we want available in our local stores. Even if something does not grow or cannot be found within 100 miles, we still expect to have access to whatever we want, whenever we want it. But the people of Cragg's cabin had to use what was in their backyard, what they could haul from the streams or lakes. The land was their home and their resource. Talk about this with your grandchildren. There are many movements today to have people buy local produce, to learn to live with their local resources and to be less dependent upon foreign products. The stories of the people who settled these prairies are filled with lessons, even if we do not want to go back in time.

Does a simple life mean a poor life? Help your grandchildren understand the riches of a full life, a simple life, and a life that collects experience, rather than goods.

A word to the wise:

Cabin Festival in June is a day of old time crafts, games for kids, interpreters in costume, and wagon rides. There is cider and soup warmed over the fires (it is your choice which one you drink)! Engage in the festivities and enjoy the blooms of spiderwort and penstemon. Take a walk through the butterfly enclosure too. This day has a lot of action to engage the children and the grandparents.

Age of grandchild: 8 and up

Best season: Summer

Contact:

Midewin National Tallgrass Prairie, 30239 South State Route 53, Wilmington, IL 60481 • (815) 423-6376 • www.fs.fed.us/mntp

Goose Lake Prairie State Natural Area, 5010 North Jugtown Road, Morris, IL 60450 • (815) 942-2899
http://dnr.state.il.us/lands/landmgt/parks/l&m/east/goose/home.htm

Now that I've reached the age where I need my children more than they need me, I really understand how grand it is to be a grandmother. Mrs. Margaret Whitlam

I & M Canal and
Great River Trails

The I & M Canal and the Great River Trail are two magnificent biking options in one of the most ambitious bike projects among the fifty states. The Grand Illinois Trail is a 475-mile trail through northern Illinois that will link Lake Michigan with the Mississippi River and connect metropolitan Chicago, Rockford and the Quad Cities with rural communities, state parks and other Illinois attractions. Two of the premier sections of this great undertaking include the great rivers of the state.

Families who choose the Illinois and Michigan Canal trail will follow a path that connects the Chicago and Illinois rivers and a canal where large barges were pulled by mules that walked along a pathway. Morris celebrates this mule/boat history in its park and statuary. The trail crosses dams and bridges, and goes along historic locks. There are no hills so the pedaling is easy and the combinations of parks that dot the trail make it a fun family outing.

This area is an outdoor museum where you can combine biking and hiking with picnics in the parks and fishing in the stream. Historic sites to include are the Gaylord Building in Lockport with a visitor center, gallery and restaurant; lock tender's house at Channahon State Park—now the park ranger home; the Dresden Village Site east of Aux Sable Aqueduct and off cemetery road. The Dresden site includes the trail's only mule barn, a former tavern, and an old cemetery.

The Great River Trail is another flat and easy trail for grandparents and grandchildren, with a variety of things to see and do along its historic and beautiful waterway. In Alton, the Sam Vadalabene section of the trail converges with Confluence Bikeway where the Illinois and Mississippi come together. It also connects with two of the areas most interesting locations—Pere Marquette State Park and the National Great Rivers Museum on one end and the Quad Cities and all their attractions on the other.

Biking is a great way to exercise, learn, connect with nature and learn history. These trails have it all.

Bonding and bridging:

Your ambition needs to match the skill and endurance of your grandchildren. Keep in mind that you are doing this with and for them—and if you need more or less pedaling than they do, accommodate that fact. Take a short ride with younger children and a longer ride with older kids.

Pack a lunch, bring a camera, stop and reflect and relax. A trail is an adventure, not just a connection between starting and stopping. Make it interesting and share your love of a silent sport, the satisfaction of using your own power to move, and a speed that allows you to observe and share.

A word to the wise:

There are wonderful options for taking young children on your bike. Kate has an old fashioned "bugger" (trailer) that fastens to your frame and makes a carriage for the child—hers will hold two. They look backward as they ride.

Now there are attachable seats that are very similar to the safety seats we use in our cars. They fasten to the handlebars and frame, and the child is between your arms and facing forward as you pedal.

A third option is a bike attachment (trailer bikes or tag-a-longs) that puts an extra wheel and seat behind your bike. This is like creating a tandem, but designed for smaller pedalers.

Age of grandchild: toddler and up

Best season: September

Contact:

Illinois and Michigan Canal Trail, PO Box 272, Morris, IL 60450 (815) 942-0796 • http://dnr.state.il.us/lands/landmgt/parks/i&m/main.htm

Illinois Department of Transportation, 2300 South Dirksen Parkway, Springfield, IL 62764 • (217) 782-7820
www.il.gov/bikemap/bikehome.html

Also check out:

Tunnel Hill State Trail;
http://dnr.state.il.us/lands/landmgt/parks/r5/tunnel.htm

Robert McClory Bike Path, Cook County Line to Wisconsin

Sunshine is delicious, rain is refreshing, wind braces us up, snow is exhilarating; there's really no such thing as bad weather, only different kinds of good weather. JOHN RUSKIN

Ulysses S. Grant Home

There are many colorful and unique towns along the Mississippi and spread throughout Illinois, but there are many reasons why Galena, with 85% of its buildings on the National Historic Register, continues to be the favorite of so many people and continues to rank with the most popular destinations.

Start your exploration at Ulysses S. Grant's home. This fine historic building is part of a complex of homes and stores that overlook the town and valley of Galena. Now a designated state historic site, this is where one of the Civil War's most famous generals and ex-president lived after the Civil War. Considering how few presidents we have had in our history, it is a rare opportunity to be in one of their homes.

Grant came to Galena to seek his fortune in 1860 after 15 years in the military and six years of limited business success. At first he rented a modest brick home and worked in his father's store as a traveling salesmen with hopes of finding a good income and a base for developing his career. Then in 1861 the war drew him back into the military where his successes inspired the town to give him this wonderful new home that he occupied until his presidency.

You can explore the Grant historic house, the neighboring Washburne House, and the Old Market House and then walk to the hill in front of the Grant House to take in the magnificent valley before descending to the historic main street.

This is a river and a hill town, founded on the lead mines that give it the name Galena (lead sulphide) and access to the Mississippi River. This was a boom town with as many as fifteen steamboats moored at the docks in the summer. The tourism of that era led to the beautiful DeSoto House which has been refurbished and is the state's oldest operating hotel.

Visit the homes, see the architecture and then complete your day with a walk or bike ride on the 3.4 mile crushed rock Galena River Trail to see the beauty that lies at the core of the community's appeal today and in the past.

Bonding and bridging:

What is history? How do we know what is historic during our lifetimes? Talk about what it means to be surrounded by buildings from the early 1800s and share what makes them special for your grandchildren. Then ask them what old is. As the "old people" in their lives we touch on the concept of old.

Then talk about the old structures that were here before the Europeans settled—places like Cahokia, just downstream on the Mississippi where a city existed before Columbus set foot on his sailing ship.

Help your grandchild understand that history is in each passing moment.

A word to the wise:

On Saturdays during the summer there is a Farmers' Market at the Market House. This is a wonderful event in any community but is truly a throwback of historic tradition that is very special in this building. Visit the booths, buy and try some of their products and help your grandchildren celebrate the tradition of American agriculture. These will be local products and many are also organic. Healthy food and an historic tradition combine in this experience.

Age of grandchild: 10 and up

Best season: Summer

Contact:

Galena State Historic Sites, PO Box 333, Galena, IL 61036 • (815) 777-3310 • www.granthome.com

Galena, IL • (877) Go Galena • www.galena.org • www.cityofgalena.org

Grant as president
www.nps.gov/history/history/online_books/presidents/site17.htm

Also check out:

Ronald Reagan Boyhood Home and Visitor Center, Dixon; (815) 288-5176; www.ronaldreaganhome.com

National Mississippi River Museum & Aquarium

Ignore the fact that this is not in East Dubuque. You do have to cross the river and technically you are in Iowa, but how can you quibble, because this is the perfect place to start an exploration of the Mississippi River and it is uniquely located right at the beginning of Illinois' 583 mile long border with the Great River. The ecology is a maze of terrestrial and aquatic life forms and a great place to begin to study Illinois.

The Mississippi is so significant to the U.S. The watershed drains 41% of the continental United States including thirty-one states and 2 Canadian provinces. And if that is not enough, the total area drained is between 1.2 and 1.8 million square miles. At New Orleans, the average flow rate is 600,000 cubic feet per second. Add to this the extraordinary wildlife diversity in and along the river—260 fish species or more than 25% of U.S. species.

The National Museum and Aquarium seeks to bring the diverse stories that summarize the unique legends and history of the river in dynamic and lively exhibits that engage both generations. Aquariums are always fascinating and these are particularly effective because they represent the world right outside the building. Here are gar and paddlefish, as well as gigantic catfish, buffalo head and carp. These are impressive and easy to see in the aquarium.

In addition, exhibits help you understand fresh water mussels—clams in the ocean. These animals were eaten, their shells were used in jewelry by the indigenous people, and later, collected to make buttons in factories all along the river valley. There are 38 species in the upper Mississippi and as many as 60 in the lower half.

The human story is not missing from this excellent museum. There is a pilot house to help you understand how barges move through the river, as well as a riverboat museum that captures the grandeur of these vessels. Riverboats were a floating hotel, gambling hall, entertainment emporium, and cargo vessel all rolled into one. Think of the magnificent paddlewheel, the steam rising, the whistle blowing and live music coming into an otherwise sleepy river town.

Bonding and bridging:

Outside you can view boats and boat parts in the Pfohl boat yards, an historic part of the Dubuque harbor. Kids can walk among the large artifacts and climb on a raft in the children's play area. Everything here adds experience and knowledge.

Walk the outside exhibits and observe the natural wetlands to understand how the system has functioned since the time of the glaciers. The Museum emphasizes care for the land as a way to protect the river and it helps you round out an excellent visit before exploring the river yourself.

After your visit, walk on the trail system that leads from the Museum and past the casino to see the river. Talk about the water and what it means. Could you drink that water? Are we taking care of this resource the way we should?

A word to the wise:

There are many ways to learn about the Mississippi, but hopefully you will find a way to go out on a boat. The Museum offers a bed and breakfast option on the William Black, a national landmark dredge vessel that is nearly as big as a football field. Imagine staying on board overnight and then having breakfast in the galley the next morning.

Age of grandchild: 5 and up

Best season: Summer

Contact: National Mississippi River Museum & Aquarium, 350 East 3rd Street, Port of Dubuque, Dubuque, IA 52001 • (563) 557-9545 www.rivermuseum.com

Mississippi River; www.greatriver.com

Also check out:

The National Great Rivers Museum, Alton; (877) 462-6979; www.greatriverroad.com/Cities/EAlton/riverMuseum.htm

There is no other door to knowledge than the door Nature opens. And there is no truth but the truth we discover in Nature. LUTHER BURBANK

Rock Island Arsenal Museum

The Rock Island Arsenal is not a relic of the past, it just has a long history that dates back to the Civil War and continues to be relevant today. You have to get a pass to get in the Arsenal, but that is not hard since you have a U.S. drivers license and a destination, but it does add to the excitement for the grandchild if they have never been on a base. The entire island (946 acres) in the Mississippi River is an active army base and a National Historic

Landmark. Acquired from the Sauk and Mesquakie Indians in 1804, it was set aside as a military reserve in 1809 and became an arsenal during the Civil War in 1862.

Get a map and listen to the directions because it is easy to get lost among all the buildings. The Arsenal Museum, established in 1905, is one of the oldest museums in the region. Inside there are the weapons and ammunition of the U.S. military from the Battle of the Little Bighorn to Desert Storm, with some arms set up in unique displays that come off the battlefield. There is even a stuffed horse, so the cavalry is represented as well.

One side note that was a surprise to us was the story of Rock Island as a military prison for Confederate soldiers. It was the northern equivalent to Andersonville according to one display. It shows how far the war reached up into the Great Lake states.

The Museum has a limited interactive area for children where the combination of old uniforms the kids can try on will be great fun for them. Where they will probably have the most fun is at the park where the larger weapons are displayed. Here are the tanks and cannons, the large caliber arsenal of weapons that are essential to ground troops.

In both the Park and the Museum there is a strong representation of American soldiers and the conditions that changed from one engagement to the next. It is a realistic look at military life.

There's a playground to help release energy.

Bonding and bridging:

If you have a background in guns and military this is a place for you, but even if you are a pacifist, the overwhelming sense of weaponry and power on display here speaks volumes about the history of conflict that has always been part of the U.S. from the early colonial wars to Iraq. All of us have had relatives in one of the twentieth century wars and even if we are seeking peace in our lifetime, we must still understand and honor those who took up arms with the hope that they were saving the country and its citizens from harm and future battles.

Visiting this place in the midst of active duty operations is a powerful experience with a lot of perspectives to share.

A word to the wise:

You have probably heard the axiom about turning swords into plowshares. Across the bridge is the John Deere Pavilion with its wonderful world of tractors, plows, and agricultural history. The invention of the steel plow was the weapon needed to open the agricultural landscape to farming; you can explore how much has changed in our world of civilian mechanization, too. Perhaps it is a chance to explore the idea of "turning swords into plowshares" and the origin of that old saying.

Age of grandchild: 10 and up

Best season: Summer

Contact: Rock Island Arsenal, 1 Rock Island Arsenal, Rock Island, IL 61299
(309) 782-5021 • http://riamwr.com

Also check out:

Chanute Aerospace Museum, Rantoul; (217) 893-1613; www.aeromuseum.org

Warbird Heritage Museum, Waukegan; (847) 244-8701; www.warbirdheritagefoundation.org

Illinois State Military Museum, Springfield; (217) 761-3910; www.il.ngb.army.mil/Museum/default.htm

One of the most powerful handclasps is that of a new grandbaby around the finger of a grandfather. Joy Hargrove

Quad City Botanical Center

Located on the banks of the Mississippi, next to the Convention Center, across the river from the arsenal, and just down the road from John Deere Pavilion, the Quad City Botanical Center is a big surprise!

A small facility with big dreams, the Botanical Center begins with a wonderful building that is imaginative and quite inviting. Set along the river, it is a dramatic addition to the city. The building welcomes you to discovery, but there is more: you can go inside and experience a tropical rain forest, a fourteen foot waterfall, banana plants, and cocoa! It is a place that changes with the seasons because it is a living museum with butterfly, conifer, and perennial gardens to explore on the outside of the building.

On dreary, grey days of November and March when you need some green, this is the place to be. Tour guides can lead you through, or you can grab a scavenger hunt form and head in for a shared adventure with your grandchildren. The scavenger hunt is a subtle, but effective way to get the child looking more closely at the plants, animals, and setting. Of course you will want some food for the Koi, because this roiling mass of colorful fish will delight your grandchild when they swirl around the food pellets.

Outside in the warmer seasons is a pleasant, calm garden, a mix of trees, water garden, and flower displays with benches for relaxing. The children will like the scrambled alphabet garden too—a nice touch for children who are proudly building their knowledge. Overall, the outdoor area is a nice place for grandparents to catch a breath after you have visited the tractors, the military, and the zoo at the other area attractions.

There are plans to have a Children's Garden in the next few years with floral displays around small buildings and fairytale settings. They also have plans for a Shakespeare Sonnet Garden.

To add to the fun, try timing your visit with one of their special events—there are monthly programs for families—"seedlings" are 5–10 years old, "little sprouts" are 3–5, and the "Starbucks" lectures are for the older audience.

Bonding and bridging:

Hiking along the Mississippi River pathways gives a sense of the forest and plants of the river flood-plains and valley. They make a tremendous contrast with the rainforest inside the garden and the plants outside the building. When we travel we look for differences and the different feelings we get are related to the vegetation. Ask your grandchild to describe a desert, a forest, a grassland—each is so different because the conditions are so different. Those conditions, which we call climate, affect both what grows there naturally and what we have to do to live there and grow our gardens.

A word to the wise:

A visit to the Niabi Zoo is a good follow up to this location. There you will have a chance to see animals that do not live in our forests and fields. Is it because of the difference in food, temperature, rainfall, and vegetation? The two stops complement one another and make a good full day of discovery and science. They also have education stops where zoo educators bring out birds, snakes, and non-living artifacts.

Age of grandchild: 3 and up

Best season: Summer

Contact: Quad City Botanical Center, 2525 4th Avenue, Rock Island, IL 61201 • (309) 794-0991 • www.qcgardens.com

Also check out:

Morton Arboretum, Lisle; (630) 968-0074; www.mortonarb.org

Anderson Japanese Gardens, Rockford; (815) 229-9390; www.andersongardens.org/

Klehm Arboretum, Rockford; (815) 965-8146; www.klehm.org

Washington Park, Springfield; www.springfieldparks.org

Luthy Botanical Garden, Peoria; (309) 686-3362; www.peoriaparks.org/luthy/luthymain.html

Chicago Botanic Garden, Glencoe; (847) 835-5440; www.chicagobotanic.org

Everyone needs to have access both to grandparents and grandchildren in order to be a full human being. Margaret Mead

John Deere Pavilion

You don't have to be a farmer to be enthralled by tractors. This attraction seems to be in the genes of grandfathers (at least the ones we know), and it is something that is easy to pass on to grandchildren. And if this strange vehicle has captured the imagination of anyone in your family, Moline is a "must see" destination.

John Deere's yellow and green are universal colors of immediate recognition and there are many opportunities to explore the world of tractors in the area of the John Deere Pavilion.

Just imagine as you wander here—this all began with the invention of a steel plow in John Deere's blacksmith shop in 1837! Now you will be exploring a complex that includes the Pavilion—a glass and steel visitor center with the

contrast of modern and historic vehicles, the John Deere store (beware—a lot of temptations here) and the John Deere Collector's Center which is a replica of a 1950s John Deere showroom complete with a wonderful collection of vintage tractors. The transition from plow manufacturer to tractor production began with the purchase of the Waterloo Gasoline Engine Company in 1918—see if you can find a Waterloo Boy Tractor. If you have the time and interest, you can even watch some restoration work on historic tractors as expert mechanics resurrect historic machines.

The Collector's Center has a small kid's corner with a pedal tractor to test drive and farm toys to play with, but the children will enjoy climbing into the large tractors with you, or sitting on some of the tractors that allow you to climb aboard. Every child loves to climb on these giant machines—they are almost jungle gyms to the small child and they evoke lots of creative play.

In addition to the tractors, the main pavilion has an excellent wall display about population growth which leads to many questions about the future of both farming and the planet and there are videos that give different ideas and perspectives about the land.

Bonding and bridging:

Americans have a love affair with the combustion engine and the vehicles we can build around it, but the tractor has a different feeling than the others. Maybe it's because of our connection with the land—planting, harvesting, and working in the elements—that makes the tractor special. It does not have sleek lines, it does not go fast, so why do we like them? Why do our grandchildren who live in cities love to play with tractors? Talk about the tractor, the population display, and the demands on our agriculture. If you are going to go to a Farmers' Market you might want to talk about where our food comes from and the plight of today's farms and farmland.

A word to the wise:

If you are really into tractors, and your grandchild is 13 or older, you might want to schedule a tour of the John Deere Tractor and Engine Factory. Seeing the vehicles put together will complete the experience for all of you and then if you still want more—check out the tractor pulls and the tractor events around the state on the Illinois and Indiana Antique Tractor and Gas Engine Club website or visit the other tractor and farm sites listed below.

Age of grandchild: 3 and up

Best season: Any

Contact:

John Deere Pavilion, 14700 River Drive, Moline, IL 61265
(309) 765-1000 • www.johndeerepavilion.com

Illinois & Indiana Antique Tractor and Gas Engine Club, PO Box 65, Penfield, IL 61862 • www.antiquefarm.org

Also check out:

Allis-Chalmers Museum, Paris; (217) 275-3428; http://allischalmersmuseum.com

Prairie Land Heritage Museum, Jacksonville; (217) 243-5678

American Farm Heritage Museum, Greenville; (618) 664-3050; www.americanfarmheritagemuseum.org

Through my grandmother's eyes, I can see more clearly the way things used to be, the way things ought to be, and most important of all, the way things really are. Ed Cunningham

Bishop Hill

Unlike many other historic villages, no one moved the buildings here. No one moved the citizens out. This is a real village—150 strong, a collection of businesses and historic structures and a story of immigration and religion that is unique.

You and your grandchild can enjoy this village from many angles. The first stop is a tribute to the artist Olof Krans who moved to Bishop Hill in 1850,

when he was 12, the same year the founder, Eric Jansson, was murdered. Kran's paintings capture the flavor of this community after Eric Jansson, in 1846, led a band of 400 Swedish immigrants across from New York through the Great Lakes to Chicago and then on a 160 mile hike across the state to their promised land.

At Bishop Hill his religious sect became established. The church is still there, as are the hotel and most of the main buildings of the cooperative society. The Colony Hotel, Colony Church, Bishop Hill Museum, and village park are state historic sites where you can tour the buildings and see the furniture or enjoy the shaded parkland. Stores, bakeries, restaurants and craft centers now occupy other historical sites, encircling the city park.

The limestone buildings are practical for a communal society led by one strong religious figure. These people worked hard and even though a quarter of the original group died in the first winter of hardship, by the time Bishop Hill hit its zenith, 1000 Swedes had immigrated to Illinois because of this group.

The best times for grandparents and grandchildren are during three festivals that are part of the Bishop Hill year. First is the Midsummer music festival (Midsommar Marque) in June; second is the Harvest Festival in September (Jordbruksdagarna) with harvest demonstrations, music, Colony Stew and children's games; and Lucia Nights in early December—the Festival of Lights with carolers and cookies in the shops. The energy rises, the feeling of community sharing an experience is real and your grandchildren can experience their lives within the village setting.

Bonding and bridging:

There are many religions and variations within those religions. Often those variations are led by charismatic people like Eric Janssen or Joseph Smith or Paul or Mohammed or Martin Luther. What is religion? You have your own religious beliefs and values, so you can share them in this discussion, but it might be of value to your grandchildren, if they are old enough, to talk about charisma, about religious sects, and the role of religion in this country and throughout the world. It is also a good time to talk about tolerance and the fact that the nation was founded on religious freedom, not on just one religion.

A word to the wise:

If you enjoy crafts and would like to try spinning, weaving, pottery and broom making, the August Clay and Fiber Fest is a great time to visit. Lots of hands-on activities and a soup supper. If Christmas shopping is a fun shared time, bring the grandchildren to Julmarknad—the Christmas Market at the end of November and beginning of December. Not only will you find unique Swedish gifts and foods, but your grandchildren will also encounter costumed Swedish folk characters wandering among the shops.

Age of grandchild: All

Best season: Midsummer and Christmas season

Contact: Bishop Hill Museum, Site Manager, PO Box 104, Bishop Hill, IL 61419 • (309) 927-3345 • www.bishophillartscouncil.com • www.bishophill.com

Also check out:

Nauvoo; www.beautifulnauvoo.com

Arthur; www.arthuril.com

Arcola; www.arcolachamber.com

Nauvoo

Nauvoo is a beautiful location on the bluffs of the Mississippi River with a memorable name and an even more unique history. A visit to the city is a chance to explore one of the most dramatic stories in Illinois history. It was here that Joseph Smith, the founder of the Church of Latter Day Saints, known as Mormons, settled with his followers.

At one time this town, whose name in Hebrew means—Beautiful Place—was the largest community in Illinois. When 5,000 Mormons arrived in 1839, the

old town of Commerce was overwhelmed, as well as renamed. Today, their history is found in a very modern Visitor Center and the surrounding brick buildings that reflect the use of the local resources of the river valley, as well as fine craftsmanship. These buildings are unique and well kept, and Mormons have returned to the community to tell their story about their past.

The best way to capture the story and the drama is to participate in the Nauvoo Pageant that runs for much of July into early August. With costumes and actors, the story is visual and exciting. There are bagpipes and drums and a large enthusiastic company of players who cover their migration to Nauvoo and the subsequent move to Salt Lake City that followed the arrest and murder of their founder in nearby Carthage.

The best way to follow up on the Pageant is on the horse-drawn covered wagon tours through the historic sections. This will put your grandchildren back in time and engage them in the excitement of the historic era. Then you can go to the brick making demonstrations, the crafts, the plays, the stores, and the community.

Walking through the park and the village is a great way to discover the statues sprinkled liberally throughout Nauvoo. The sculptures are life-like and dramatic, which gives an extra dimension to the discoveries of a good walking tour. In the right light and angle they almost seem to come alive. This is the magic of the community, the mix of old and new, of stories and beliefs, of discrimination and determination.

Bonding and bridging:

What makes us hate others? Why do we get upset when people believe differently than we do, when they have a different colored skin, when they speak with an accent? Why do we worship some people, envy others, and express intolerance for still others—even if we do not know them, have not met them, have no basis for our intolerance? This is a great place to talk about this important topic.

Our country is founded on freedoms, but we have terrible stories of repression of Indians, women, slaves, and religious groups who have not been allowed to access those freedoms. Is that right? Is that fair? Talk about this with your grandchildren—because you have a sense of history that they cannot grasp without your help.

A word to the wise:

This recommendation is not intended to be religious. Those who are Mormons will have a different experience than those who are not. We recommend this site because it is a powerful story and stories are the basis for our knowledge and our beliefs. So with that in mind, this community, the pageants, the interpretation, and the overall experience can be very powerful and you need to consider whether your grandchild is ready to explore this kind of experience, whether the child can absorb the history and the story without being captured by the religious fervor and recruitment that is also part of the programming.

Age of grandchild: 10 and up

Best season: Summer

Contact: Nauvoo Tourism Office, 1295 Mulholland Street, PO Box 500, Nauvoo, IL 62354 • (217) 453-6648 • (877) NAUVOO-1
www.beautifulnauvoo.com • /www.nauvoopageant.org/ • www.nauvoo.net
www.historicnauvoo.net/

Also check out:

Arthur; www.arthuril.com

Arcola; www.arcolachamber.com

Bishop Hill; www.bishophill.com

Wildlife Prairie State Park

This is not a zoo and it is not a natural landscape of native animals, it is a complex of wildlife and natural landscapes that gives the illusion of animals moving in their native habitats. Unlike a zoo, these animals have space to roam. While the animals are still confined, their confinement is not just a design for human observers, and it conveys privacy to each animal.

For species like the wild cats that are secretive and solitary, there are open places to roam, dotted with tree cover. But these hideouts are not a negative for the viewer. There are bridges and a variety of access points to get a good

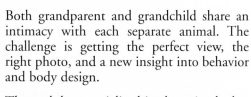

view. It is more a benign exercise in hunting and stalking, rather than just walking to a cage, looking and moving on.

Both grandparent and grandchild share an intimacy with each separate animal. The challenge is getting the perfect view, the right photo, and a new insight into behavior and body design.

The park has specialized in the animals that were historically part of Illinois, such as the wolf, bear, elk, bison, and cougar. These are animals that belong here, but just as people have brought them to this site, people have removed many of them from the wild. Although they are no longer common, you and your grandchild can explore a restored prairie and wetland, as well as woods and lake environment. There is even a butterfly garden to help you observe a small and colorful part of the summer plant community.

And what about the pioneers? They, too, have disappeared. But here is an 1800 farmstead, a one room school house, and a log cabin you can visit by foot or observe on a train ride.

It was one man's vision that created this park—William Rutherford, who died in 2006. He was the visionary who wanted to see part of our heritage preserved and he was so effective in his own life that he helped save 62,000 acres in Australia and contributed to the success of zoos and parks all over Illinois. Remember him when you walk together because he represents the good in humankind and the potential that each of us has to make a difference.

Bonding and bridging:

Are the fences to protect the people from the animals or the animals from the people? This is a good question to ask the children. Who really poses the greater danger—the animals or the humans?

Talk about the individual species and how they might have conflicted with pioneer, settler, and twentieth century cities and farms. Why do we pass laws like the Endangered Species Act and limit how many animals can be hunted and when?

What have we learned in the years since settling the continent and how are we adjusting to sharing the planet with other species? Tell them how things were when you were young. Help them see how much and how fast things are changing.

A word to the wise:

A safari might be out of your price range and a time travel machine is probably a few years off, but here are both—a walk through the Illinois past, but surrounded by life. It is an excursion that you cannot do anywhere else and to top that off you have the option of staying overnight on the prairie in a renovated caboose, or you can stay in a cabin on the hill, a cottage by the lake, or in a prairie stable. Take your time, take photos, and stay long enough to feel like you belong.

Age of grandchild: 2 and up

Best season: Spring

Contact: Wildlife Prairie State Park, 3826 North Taylor Road, Hanna City, IL 61536• (309) 676-0998 • www.wildlifeprairiestatepark.org

Also check out:

Lincoln Park Zoo, Chicago; (312) 742-2000; www.lpzoo.org

Miller Park Zoo, Bloomington; (309) 434-2509; www.cityblm.org/zoo

Brookfield Zoo, Brookfield; (708) 688-8000; www.brookfieldzoo.org

Scoville Zoo, Decatur; (217) 421-7435; www.decatur-parks.org/zoo/

Miller Park

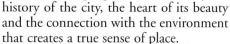

We have national and state parks that get lots of ink in publications about places you have to visit before you die, but where are the voices of advocates of city parks? We hear of Central Park and the Chicago Lakefront, but it is not just in the largest of our communities that city parks are memorable and worth a special visit. Parks like Miller in Bloomington, Laura Bradley or Glen Oaks in Peoria, and Riverview Park in Rockford are unique places that embody the

history of the city, the heart of its beauty and the connection with the environment that creates a true sense of place.

Miller Park is a wonderful combination of memorials, picnic areas, trees, recreation areas, a zoo, and a fishing pond. It is easy to get to and provides a variety of opportunities for grandparents and grandchildren.

The zoo is one of our favorites—clean, and well presented. They have resisted the temptation to try to be too much, but at the same time offer enough variety to make repeated visits worthwhile. They have managed to add a wonderful Wallaby Walk About that lets you stroll through Australia and a Tropics exhibit inspiring thoughts of rain forests and biodiversity. Nothing is too big, nothing is too crowded for good observation and contemplation. In fact, the smallness of the zoo means you can give into the temptation to see everything and then you can return to spend the time required to enjoy one of your favorite exhibits, like the active otter stream.

You can couple your visit with a picnic beneath some magnificent shade trees that include exotics like the Ginkgo. Large oaks and maples exemplify the full shape and beauty of living sculptures.

On hot days the lake is inviting, whether on the beach or the fishing dock. Water is central to everything we do and it is no less important to the park. It is aesthetic and yet recreational. You can walk around it, sit and observe, or get wet. The options are great and you only need to make sure your grandchild is safe in whichever activity they choose.

Bonding and bridging:

Are people and nature incompatible? The environment should not be in conflict with our lives, it
should be a consideration in all we do. The three
E's of all our communities are Economy, Education,
and Environment. We do best when they are blended
and enhanced. Is a community richer for having
green spaces? Do you feel different here than in the downtown or the
mall? Is it a good feeling? What can you do in the park that you can't do in
other places?

Look at the trees, flowers, birds, and squirrels. Who has lived here
longer? Do we owe a debt to the people and nature that preceded us?
How can we live in harmony with everything around us and enjoy the
richness of life?

A word to the wise:

All of us are most active when we have incentive to move and food is a great
motivator for every living thing, including us. To really enjoy your visit, time
it for feeding time—Marine Mammals at 10:30 and 3:00 and Big Cats and
Bears at 4:00. Think of how nice it is to fall asleep after a big meal. The same
is true for all animals. Come after feeding time and you can study naps!

Age of grandchild: All

Best season: Spring and summer

Contact: Miller Park Zoo, 1020 South Morris Avenue, Bloomington, IL
61701 • (309) 434-2250 • www.cityblm.org/zoo

Also check out:

Laura Bradley Park, Peoria; (800) 747-0302;
www.fermatainc.com/il/site_26.html

Riverview Park, Rockford; (815) 987-8800; www.rockfordparkdistrict.org

Glen Oaks Park, Peoria; (309) 682-1200;
www.peoriaparks.org/parks/gopark.html

*I don't intentionally spoil my grandkids. It's just that
correcting them often takes more energy than I have left.* GENE PERRET

79

Lincoln's New Salem State Historic Site

There are many historic sites where old buildings have been brought together to give us a tangible connection to other eras and life of the settlers and frontier business people. But, only New Salem can give you the additional insight of a president making his mark in the world and setting the stage for a future of leadership and challenge.

New Salem is a reconstruction of the village of Abraham Lincoln's young adulthood. This is where he developed purpose and direction in life. From here he embarked upon law and statesmanship. It was the log cabin village

that gave him the experiences that he would build upon. During his six years in New Salem he worked as a store clerk, rail splitter, soldier in the Black Hawk War, postmaster, deputy surveyor and businessman. He came in 1831 and by the time he left in 1837, he was elected to the General Assembly and moved to Springfield to begin his law career.

Today you will find a very informative Visitor Center that will set the stage for the exploration of the village and provide a short video that is important to getting the most out of your walk. This visual will help your grandchild get some of the history and add to the effectiveness of the displays.

Twelve log houses, ten workshops, stores, mills, the Rutledge Tavern, and the school where church services were also held have been reproduced by the CCC (Civilian Conservation Corps). The Onstot Cooper Shop was moved from Petersburg and is the only original building in the community.

Through donations and intense research, the buildings are furnished with authentic period pieces which will impress the grandparents, but it is probably the livestock that will catch the eye of the grandchildren.

There are many excellent interpreters who will help you understand life in New Salem. You can help by asking questions and getting your grandchildren involved with these costumed instructors.

Bonding and bridging:

Much of the history of America revolves around Lincoln. No other president has such a pivotal role, with the exception of Washington, and no president is so revered and studied. There are many museums, and almost any place he stayed has become an historic site, but this one is special. This is where you can talk about the value of getting lots of different experiences in life and how the things we do when we are young help us later as we find careers.

It is up to us to gather experiences just as Lincoln did. Talk about the different things you did when you were young—the jobs, travels, military. Challenge your grandchildren to see opportunity and to branch out and embrace new experiences. What new experiences have they already had?

A word to the wise:

Special events are the best way to really get engaged in the period and the history of any site and this location has some excellent variety in their offerings. In September the traditional music of the nineteenth century comes to New Salem. Music is essential to understanding both time and culture. In October surveyors demonstrate the same methods Lincoln used. The Candlelight Tour in October provides great atmosphere. With Militia drills, wrestling, and lots of other options, check their website and choose the experience that fits your family the best.

Age of grandchild: All

Best season: Summer

Contact: Lincoln's New Salem, 15588 History Lane, Petersburg, IL 62675
(217) 632-4000 • www.lincolnsnewsalem.com

Also check out:

Bishop Hill; www.bishophill.com

Naper Settlement; (630) 420-6010; www.napersettlement.org

The real mystery of life is not a problem to be solved, it is a reality to be experienced. J.J. Van der Leeuw

Lincoln Home
National Historic Site

Even George Washington has a hard time measuring up to the books, lore, and love that Lincoln engenders. Lincoln is the tragic figure, the father of the second sequence in the development of the United States, the liberator, the manager, the voice of reason and compassion in our bloodiest period of history and he was born and raised here in the middle of America.

Illinois is filled with Lincoln locations and all of them are worth visiting. He is an icon, not because he was president, but because, as president, he struggled with the inconsistency of a nation that was just shy of 100 years old. He was the

final arbitrator in the worst decision our founding fathers could make—the justification of slavery—and as a result he had to deal with mixed emotions and violence. There is no way to understand the complexities that he faced, the conflicting interests and opinions and the need through all of the conflict to come to a resolution that would reunite the country and right the nation's worst wrong.

This is the place to start, the place where Lincoln served as an attorney after rising from his modest log cabin beginnings. This was not a unique place; in fact, the National Monument not only captures Lincoln's home, but also a very typical quiet street in the bustle of the state capitol. It is a reflection on the time, as much as the man and place, to see how greatness cannot be predicted by location or ancestry.

With a Visitor Center to establish perspective and guides to help you understand the times, the location, and the man, it is possible for you and your family to step back in time, perhaps to note how you handle conflict, what the major issues are in your time and place, and how you address the issues of right, wrong, and ethics.

It is also a place of quiet reflection and timelessness. He lived here for seventeen years and as he left for Washington D. C., having rented the home and sold their furnishings, he stated that "… to this place, and the kindness of these people, I owe everything." His body was returned to the site as the funeral procession passed down these very same blocks you can walk.

Bonding and bridging:

A grandparent has lived through many presidents and many issues, but the grandchild often has no concept of a president. This is a time to explore the power and responsibility of leaders and governments. Talk about what it means to be a good leader.

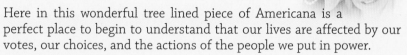

Here in this wonderful tree lined piece of Americana is a perfect place to begin to understand that our lives are affected by our votes, our choices, and the actions of the people we put in power.

A word to the wise:

A stroll down this quiet street might help you remember the small town you lived in or visited as a child. It's good to talk about the way people used to live. What were the games the children played and the work parents did? Talk about your life as a youth and how it is different from today. Time travel with one another and visit one of the programs of Park Service to help you connect with history. Finding a way to slow down the pace of life for a day or an afternoon might be one of the greatest presents you can give your grandchildren.

Age of grandchild: 5 and up

Best season: Any

Contact:

Lincoln Home National Historic Site, Visitor Center, 426 South Seventh Street, Springfield, IL 62701 • (217) 391-3226 • www.nps.gov/liho

Historic Sites in Springfield; Springfield Visitors Bureau, 109 North Seventh Street, Springfield, IL 62701 • (800) 545-7300 www.visit-springfieldillinois.com/visitor/historic.asp

Also check out:

Lincoln Courthouse, Beardstown; (217) 323-3271; www.lincolninbeardstown.org

Lincoln-Douglas Debate Museum, Charleston; (217) 348-0430

Lincoln Log Cabin State Historic Site, Lerna; (217) 345-1845; www.lincolnlogcabin.org

Lincoln's New Salem State Historic Site, Petersburg; (217) 632-4000; www.lincolnsnewsalem.com

A child needs a grandparent, anybody's grandparent, to grow a little more securely into an unfamiliar world. CHARLES AND ANN MORSE

Illinois State Capitol

We are a culture of symbols—religion, economics, and politics—and no structure is more symbolic of our democratic system than the State Capitol. Most states have undergone changes of location and buildings. Even our nation's Capitol was preceded by other buildings and locations. So, it's not unusual that Springfield has two Capitol buildings and you should visit both.

The Old State Capitol is a state historic site that was occupied from 1839–1876. Earlier statehouses existed in Kaskaskia and Vandalia. In Springfield you will find a statue of Lincoln inviting you into the building, even though he lost his battle with Stephen Douglas for a Senate seat before defeating him for an even more

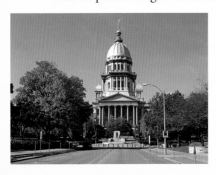

significant elected office—President. But both here and at the current Capitol it was more than famous men who served the state. In fact we have had thousands of men and women serve in state governments, most of whom are lost in anonymity after leaving office.

Like many of the Capitols all over the world, today's is located on a high point in Springfield. It had been the site of a grove of trees that were so attractive that some wanted to have Lincoln buried here. This was to be Illinois' sixth Capitol. The building was designed by the Chicago-based architectural firm of Cochrane and Garnsey, and approved by the General Assembly. There is some controversy about who should actually be credited with the design since J. C. Cochrane took the credit, but most of the work was actually done by George Garnsey and Alfred Piquenard.

The building should be seen from both inside and outside to get a sense of its timelessness. Walk up the central mall through the parkland and statuary. Maybe pay homage to a couple of statues and paintings and discuss how people have used these common grounds for protests, rallies, and demonstrations, and how those acts are the basis for democracy. Let your grandchild know that this is their Capitol—the people in it are their representatives, and the right to assemble and disagree is at the heart of what is America, from the Boston Tea Party to today.

Look into the chambers where the laws are passed, go into the galleries if they are in session and watch the messy process from the balcony. Stroll the halls, find your Senator and go next door and find your Representative. You can wander on your own, but there are regular tours every day. Groups must make reservations in advance.

Bonding and bridging:

The lesson that you can impart from your own history is that it is the people who can make a difference in this country. The building is in essence, yours. These are your employees and it is your responsibility to make sure that they are doing a good job or you vote them out. Is there any more important lesson that we can impart to our grandchildren? Democracy works only when individuals make their voice heard.

Ask your grandchildren what they think is important in the world and help them draft a letter to their Senator or Representative. Show them how to participate in government.

Here is the place to begin. Tell stories—don't lecture. Share history. Take another walk around the grounds after the tour. Find out who we thought was significant enough to have a statue, visit the war memorials, and go to the Illinois Museums.

A word to the wise:

Make an appointment to visit your Senator and Representative. Even if you know them at home, they look different in their offices. Get a photo taken. Be prepared with a few good questions so the conversation doesn't lag, but do not make this a lobbying visit.

Age of grandchild: 12 and up

Best season: Winter when they are in session, or in the summer when you can walk in the park.

Contact:

The Illinois State Capitol, Second and Capitol, Springfield, IL
(217) 782-2099 • www.online-springfield.com/sites/capitol.html •
www.ilstatehouse.com

Learn Illinois Capitols website
www.state.il.us/kids/learn/capitols/default.htm

Also check out:

Kaskaskia; www.greatriverroad.com/stegen/randattract/kaskaskia.ht

Vandalia; www.vandaliaillinois.com/oldstatecapital.html

Illinois State Museum

What do we know about Illinois? Land of Lincoln, can't miss that one—it's on every license plate. It is home to Chicago, the Cubs, White Sox, Bears, Black Hawks, and Bulls. We even know that Springfield is the capital and Lincoln lived here. But there are some things most people don't know, like the fact that this wonderful museum is right next door to the capitol. And did you know that Illinois was once south of the equator? Sounds crazy, but the proof is here in the exhibit, "Changes, Dynamic Illinois Environments."

The State Museum is a dynamic place to put Illinois in perspective. It belongs to everyone and it strives to tell stories in picturesque and captivating ways. Walking through the Changes exhibit is a 500,000 year stroll, compressed for

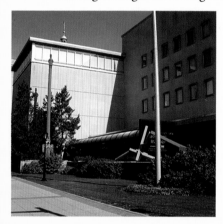

your convenience. The dioramas are distinct and artful, creating a nice scenic walk, but the incorporation of the senses is most enjoyable. You can engage with interactive displays to explore the areas you and your grandchildren find most interesting.

Travel through a mine and a glacial tunnel, then touch a cave bear's skull, listen to the account of an early traveler on the Illinois River, and get weather reports from a million years ago. Then if you have become curious about the world and want to enjoy the quest for knowledge that brought these artifacts and information together, you can explore the illuminated drawers, and unique mini-displays that allow you to test your own knowledge and skills. See the land before people arrived and learn about how people altered the land. Learn about the aboriginal people and the recent immigrants in this all inclusive walk.

In the "At Home in the Heartlands" section you learn about people of the past, including their stories. Then you can see the massive paper weights collection and wonder what motivates the collecting instinct in all of us. Move to the downstairs children's area called "A Place for Discovery". Here are hands-on art works and opportunities to explore the museum world in a very personal way.

Bonding and bridging:

History. How many of us remember yawning in history class? Memorizing dates and names of ancient explorers had so little to do with our lives that the information went in one ear and out the other. A museum like this can create excitement and curiosity about the past like the classroom can never do.

Talk with your grandchild (assuming they're old enough to remember) about events that have been important to them. Was it the first day of school, the holidays, the house that they live in? If they're old enough, this would be a good time to show them a family tree, with a photo album of pictures of those ancestors. Sometimes we can see resemblances to people who lived long before us.

A word to the wise:

The second Saturday of each month the Discovery Center has a special program especially geared for ages 4–8. These include take home crafts that take about 30–45 minutes to complete, and best of all, they encourage parents and grandparents to participate. In the summer they have a free children's film series that includes a variety of topics and cartoons. Call for schedules and reservations.

Age of grandchild: All

Best season: All, but especially good for hot days, rainy days or cold days.

Contact: Illinois State Museum, 502 South Spring Street, Springfield, IL 62706 • (217) 782-7386 • www.museum.state.il.us

Also check out:

Lockport Gallery, Lockport; (815) 838-7400; www.museum.state.il.us/ismsites/lockport

Dickson Mounds Museum, Lewistown; (309) 547-3721; www.museum.state.il.us/ismsites/dickson

Chicago Gallery and Artisans Shop, Chicago; (312) 814-5322; www.museum.state.il.us/ismsites/chicago

Southern Illinois Artisans Shop and Art Gallery, Whittington; (618) 629-2220; www.museum.state.il.us/ismsites/so-il

If I had known how wonderful it would be to have grandchildren, I'd have had them first. Lois Wyse

Abraham Lincoln Presidential Library and Museum

A visit to Springfield absolutely must include a visit to the Abraham Lincoln Presidential Library and Museum. This 21st century facility is unlike other scholarly museums you may encounter. What makes this Museum unique are all the special effects, including holography, interactive displays, multimedia programs and lifelike mannequins in numerous tableaus throughout the Museum.

As you enter and walk down a wide corridor to the Museum proper you will see the Lincoln family ahead of you, gathered together as if in preparation for a formal portrait. You and your grandchild can stand next to any of them and have your picture taken. Behind them is a replica of the 1861 White House with important historical characters standing about, including John Wilkes Booth who leans against a column with arms crossed.

Inside the White House is a room filled with formal gowns, and Mary stands on a raised platform in the center of the room being fitted. Many of the characters have such true-to-life facial expression and body posture that you expect them to turn their heads as you pass by. They also give emotional feeling—especially the Slave Auction and Mary Lincoln in mourning the death of one of her sons. There is intensity and seriousness in some of the exhibits.

But all is not gloom and doom. The use of Holovision in the Ghosts of the Library will have you staring with disbelief as ghostly images appear and disappear. In the Union Theater, automated special effects will have you sitting on the edge of your seat and maybe even lifting off momentarily, with the realistic sounds and shudder of cannon fire. Another room has a wall of TVs reporting on Lincoln's 1860 campaign, as if it were taking place in our own time, complete with campaign commercials.

In an interactive exhibit, you can ask questions of the President. You must choose one from a pre-selected list and then you enter the small viewing area where Lincoln's voice responds to your question, and if you don't believe the answer, his library is across the street.

Bonding and bridging:

Most of us have parts of our past that we are not proud of, when we didn't live up to our own expectations. The same is true of our country and certainly slavery is our most serious failing as a democracy. A visit to the Lincoln Memorial is a time to talk about individual courage and convictions.

We all know our grandchildren will face crisis and doubt in their lives and we need to reassure them when they are young that dealing honestly with these kinds of struggles makes us stronger. It is important to remind our grandchildren that even someone of Abe's stature had weaknesses, but he made the world a better place as a result.

A word to the wise:

If you have grandchildren younger than school age, they will be fascinated by some of the displays and possibly frightened by others (The Union Theater and the Ghosts of the Library shows), but they will thoroughly enjoy themselves in Mrs. Lincoln's Attic, where they can dress up in period costumes, scribble with chalk on a slate board, pretend to cook a meal and play with reproduction toys and dollhouse.

You should also know that weekdays at certain times of the year, bus loads of school kids will be coming to the Museum, so you might want to call ahead to find out if it is a particularly large attendance day. Crowded spaces make it harder for smaller grandchildren to see all of the displays and exhibits.

Age of grandchild: 5 and up

Best season: All

Contact: Abraham Lincoln Presidential Library and Museum, 212 North Sixth Street, Springfield, IL 62701 • (217) 558-8844 or (800) 610-2094 • www.alplm.org

Also check out:

Illinois State Museum, Springfield; (217) 782-7386; www.museum.state.il.us

Chicago History Museum, Chicago; (312) 642-4600; www.chicagohistory.org

Ronald Reagan boyhood home, Dixon; (815) 288-5176; www.rambletherock.com/reagan.htm

Family faces are magic mirrors. Looking at people who belong to us, we see the past, present and future. GAIL LUMET BUCKLEY

Chanute Aerospace Museum

To fly like the birds has been a dream of humans ever since we learned that our bodies were pretty tightly held to the earth. For centuries people imagined human flight and Leonardo da Vinci actually came up with some very good designs, but it wasn't until our own grandparents were young that the dream became reality.

How old were you when you went on your first airplane ride? Many of today's grandkids have already logged thousands of miles before their first birthday. Certainly airplanes are not something they are surprised to see, yet we all still

thrill to see just what these flying machines can do. Located in a portion of a closed U.S. Air Force base, the non-profit museum provides a wonderful history of aviation and the Air Force. The Museum is named for Octave Chanute, a contemporary of Orville and Wilbur Wright who created a bi-winged glider at age 64 and flew it on more than 1000 manned flights near Gary, Indiana—without an accident. A replica of the glider is one of the features of the Museum, along with models of the Wright Brothers airplane and Lindbergh's Spirit of St. Louis.

The Museum provides a timeline of aviation history including flight in the World Wars and the Tuskegee Airmen. Kids will like all the model airplanes in the display cases, as well as the walk among the fighters and bombers that are both inside and out. It is quite a jump from glider to barnstormer to military and commercial jets—growth in aviation built on early designs, so both the Wrights and Chanute put the early bolts on today's aircraft.

Consider combining your visit with the summer Air Festival. Airplanes of all shapes, sizes, and vintages are spread across the grounds, but the real highlight is the afternoon air shows. Bring along a blanket or folding chairs and find a spot on the grass next to the airstrip. Single engine planes fly solo, doing 'loop de loops,' squadrons of biplanes do synchronized dives and barrel rolls, and daredevil wing walkers somehow stay on board even as the plane flies upside down. Huge military transports stun us with their size and maneuverability.

Bonding and bridging:

Dreams—both those at night and during our waking hours have an impact on our lives. Have you ever had a dream where you were actually flying? Has your grandchild? What about our daydreams? Is flying an airplane something either one of you has dreamed about doing? For your grandchild, this could be a possibility. With any such dream, there has to be an accompanying effort—studying, saving money, or working with others already living the dream. Share with your grandchildren a dream you had as a child. Let them know that dreams do come true, for those who hold to them.

A word to the wise:

It is easy to get caught up in the dramatic shape of the military jets, but help your grandchildren get the experience of wondering about the early forms of flight as well. Build their knowledge by making a model plane or flying a kite. Our grandchildren love the simple balsa gliders and the fact that they can actually make something fly.

Age of grandchild: 9 and up

Best season: All, but the air festival is in summer

Contact:

Chanute Aerospace Museum, 1011 Pacesetter Drive, Rantoul, IL 61866 (217) 893-1613 or 1-877-RANTOUL • www.aeromuseum.org/

Also check out:

Air Classics Museum of Aviation, Sugar Grove; www.airclassicsmuseum.org

Greater St. Louis Air & Space Museum, Cahokia; www.airandspacemuseum.org/

Heritage In Flight Museum, Lincoln; www.heritageinflight.org

Prairie Aviation Museum, Bloomington; www.prairieaviationmuseum.org

Warbird Heritage Museum, Waukegan; www.warbirdheritagefoundation.org

World Aerospace Museum, Quincy; www.jet-warbirds.com

Bringing up a family should be an adventure, not an anxious discipline in which everybody is constantly graded for performance. MILTON R. SAPERSTEIN

Wandell Sculpture Garden

Meadowbrook Park in Urbana is the ultimate urban park complex in one 130 acre complex that celebrates nature, artistic expression, and living in the city. Families fill every part of the park, enjoying the diverse settings and the creative landscape.

The first thing you see is a wonderful sculpture of two hammers facing one another. These immense hammers are whimsical, colorful and just the right touch for the picnic area and playground. Called the Prairieplay Playground, kids find lots of challenges for climbing, sliding, swinging and exploring. Next to it is the Prairieplay Picnic Pavilion where you can enjoy an outdoor meal, or sit and observe your grandchildren play.

Near the playground is the restored prairie, a dynamic system that recalls the open landscape that greeted the American Indians, the pioneers, and the explorers as they wandered in early Illinois. This landscape is filled with flowers throughout the summer and breezes ripple the tall grasses like waves on a lake.

Connecting the two parts of the park are more playful sculptures; part of the Wandell Sculpture Garden is concentrated within one area of the park, but spills out along the pathways and natural landscapes with humor and artistry. These sculptures blend with the natural setting and occasionally surprise you with their color, subject or shape. These works, created by internationally prominent sculptors, change over time, giving the park a sense of new discovery each year. But they also give the trail an extra vitality for your walk with your grandchild. As you walk through the prairie and listen for bird songs or catch a glimpse of a new flower, you know that your grandchild is already anticipating another sculpture and therefore motivated to keep walking on the three miles of paved trails.

And if that is not enough to give you and your grandchildren both exercise and inspiration, the loop trail also goes through the Timpone Ornamental Tree Grove, a sensory garden, the Hickman Wildflower Walk, an herb garden, a windmill garden, and the Walker Grove savanna!

Just make sure you have lots of time and liquids to enjoy this outstanding park.

Bonding and bridging:

What is beautiful? What is art? It is hard to answer these questions. Kids love to create things and it would be good to bring some basic art supplies for painting and clay for sculpting if you want to explore the idea of art with the child. They do not know that they are making representative or abstract art as their figures and shapes conform to an inner idea about what they are seeing. As the children grow, you can take them further into the ideas of creativity, form, and design.

A word to the wise:

The Sensory Garden is a wonderful place for interactive learning. The variety of plants are grouped together because they have special textures, smells, colors, taste, and even sound. Next to the corn crib and the Windmill Garden this garden fills the children with curiosity and can begin to teach them about both plants and gardens.

The world of plants is one of endless variety and surprise and you can help your grandchildren explore this by including the Herb Garden too. Bring along some bottles of kitchen spice and let the children compare the plant source with the commercial bottle. It is nice for them to learn that foods we buy do not start out in bottles and cans.

Age of grandchild: All

Best season: Summer

Contact: Meadowbrook Park, Race Street and Windsor Road, Urbana, IL 61801 • (217) 367-1544 • www.urbanaparks.org
www.sculpture.org/documents/parksdir/p&g/wandell/wand.shtml

Also check out:

Skokie Northshore Sculpture Park, Skokie; (847) 679-4265; www.sculpturepark.org

Wood Street Gallery and Sculpture Garden, Des Plaines; (773) 227-3306; www.sculpture.org/documents/parksdir/usa/midwest.shtml

Busey Woods and Anita Purvis Nature Center; http://www.urbanaparks.org/facilities/32.html

The closest friends I have made all through life have been people who also grew up close to a loved and living grandmother or grandfather. Margaret Mead

Amish Country:
Arthur and Arcola

The Amish have a long history that includes terrible stories of martyrs and prejudice, but today they are perhaps a source of curiosity to an American public that cannot understand forsaking cars and the other accoutrements of our culture and time. The image of the Amish is centered on their horses and buggies as much as their simple clothing and seemingly historic lifestyle. But there is much to explore and learn from the people and this area is the fourth largest Amish concentration in the country, behind Pennsylvania, Indiana, and Ohio. The best place to begin is at the Amish Interpretive Center in Arcola where a short video complements a museum of Amish culture that allows you to share this simple life with your grandchildren.

This is a wonderful place to see the "plain people." Started by Jakob Ammann, a seventeenth century Mennonite elder, the Amish group believes that simplicity of living and detachment from the world are the keys to salvation, but their lifestyle created many misconceptions. The three men who started the Interpretive Center felt it was time to separate fact from myth. Here you can see the quilts, the basic furnishings of the home, examples of the clothing and even the toys of the Amish children. This will fascinate your grandchildren who may think that this is an historic museum, instead of a museum of the present.

Drive the countryside and see the homes, the families working their farms, the horse-drawn buggies riding down the road and clothing hanging on the line to dry. See an Amish school where children go through eight grades with math, social studies, spelling, writing, health and German as their first language. They do not learn science, but they do learn to drive a horse and buggy. You might also note a very large green "church" wagon outside a home. This identifies the home as the location for the next church service, and the hymnals and other service materials are inside.

Finally, you should take the children to Arthur where there is an Amish bakery and Amish products in many shops. You can also buy lunch at Yoder's Kitchen where the menu features Amish/Mennonite cooking. If possible, make the visit during Arthur Days. The Arthur Cheese Festival brings together thousands of people for a Labor Day Weekend that includes huge cheese wheels, a National Cheese Curling contest, cheese eating contests, and games.

Bonding and bridging:

Sometimes technology and pace can get to be too
much! You probably already share some concern
about shaping your grandchildren's perspective.
This trip is one chance to question if we really
need technology or if it is something we can choose.
Do we have to have what our friends have, or can we
choose experiences that are simple, but fun? What we remember about
our own grandparents are the many times shared. Ask your grandchildren about any fun times they remember playing simple games like
Jacks, marble games or playing with magnets.

A word to the wise:

You are showing them a world that is slower paced, so make sure you keep to
a slow pace too. Have a picnic in the Arthur Park, drive slow so you do not
endanger the buggies and their passengers. Take photos, but be respectful and
avoid taking photos of the Amish that will show their faces—they do not like
this and you should respect that. Do not go on their property or stop and
gawk. Do not try to feed their horses when they are "parked."

Age of grandchild: 5 to 12

Best season: All

Contact:

Arthur, IL • www.arthuril.com

Arcola, IL • www.arcolachamber.com

Also check out:

Bishop Hill; www.bishophill.com or www.bishophillartscouncil.com

Nauvoo; www.beautifulnauvoo.com

Raggedy Ann & Andy Museum and Festival

List the toys you had that are the same as the toys your grandchildren have. Not a very long list, but for many of us, Raggedy Ann & Andy are on this short list. They still calm, satisfy and comfort generation after generation, with no end in sight. So with this common ground, how could you not visit the Raggedy Ann & Andy Museum in Arcola?

This is the birthplace of Johnny Gruelle, a freelance artist and political and sports cartoonist. The emphasis of the museum is Johnny's illustrating and cartoon drawing that formed the creative basis for Raggedy Ann and later Andy. The first books came out in 1918 and by 1922 the stories of these dolls were in magazines; in 1934 his illustrated Raggedy Ann proverbs were in national syndication. Raggedy Ann has been named to the Toy Hall of Fame and hopefully Andy will join her soon.

Johnny died in 1938, but his creation promises to live on through many more generations. This was the idea of Joni Wannamaker, Johnny's granddaughter and Arcola resident when she created the Raggedy Ann & Andy Museum. It is nostalgic for the grandparents, a wonder for the grandchild. Dolls of all sizes fill the rooms. Raggedy Ann & Andy images are everywhere and there are murals and supporting characters, like the camel with the wrinkled knees. Included is a wonderful painting and doll collection that shows the great fondness many Japanese have for the dolls, including an annual celebration of Ann and Andy. Hard to believe, but the posters show how loved they are.

The origin of Ann, the first of the two dolls, is clouded in some myth. According to one story, the doll belonged to Johnny's mother, and his daughter Marcella carried it into his studio during an afternoon in 1914. Johnny drew a smile on the face and added two round black buttons. Using two poems—The Raggedy Man and Little Orphan Annie—for inspiration, the doll got her name. Publishing a Raggedy Ann book every year for twenty years, he honored his daughter in 1929 with a book entitled *Marcella: A Raggedy Ann Story*.

Bonding and bridging:

Our toys often are a reflection of who we are and our history. Whether it is Lincoln Logs and Erector Sets or hula hoops and hobby horses, we all have favorites. Find out what your grandchildren like and share with them the toys of your childhood. Just saying names like TinkerToys, Rockem-Sockem Robots, Radio Flyers, yo-yos, GI Joe, and Slinky evokes images and laughter for many of us. What will be the toys your grandchildren will remember? We have found that often we can introduce our young grandchildren to old toys and they are just as impressed as we were. So as you talk about toys, try to find out what they enjoy about the toy. What is fun?

A word to the wise:

If you want to really make the most out of your trip – try to plan it for the Raggedy Ann & Andy festival in June. There will be a lot of people in Raggedy costumes in the parade and along the street. The porches in the community are decorated in Raggedy themes and there are stages with magic, music, and stories. Kiddie tractor pulls, jugglers, a children's parade and a Toyland parade, plus special performances are all part of the two day event.

Join in, dress up, have fun. Get your photos taken with a Raggedy Ann character, enjoy the food, check out the crafts, and have a great time together. When you participate, it is easy for your grandchildren to do so too.

Age of grandchild: 3 to 8

Best season: June is the festival, otherwise all year.

Contact:

The Raggedy Ann and Andy Museum; PO Box 183,110 East Main Street, Arcola, IL 61910 • (217) 268-4908 • www.raggedyann-museum.org

National Toy Hall of Fame; www.strongmuseum.org/NTHoF/NTHoF.html

Also check out:

American Girl Place, Chicago; (877) 247-5223; www.americangirlplace.com

National Great Rivers Museum

People tend to picture Illinois as Chicago or the great flat stretches of farm land leveled by the ancient glaciers, but only a few realize Illinois is a state of great rivers and near St. Louis, MO and Alton, IL three of the rivers converge—the Illinois, the Missouri, and the Mississippi. Along the southern border of the state is the Ohio. Four large scale rivers that reach to Pennsylvania, Yellowstone, northern Minnesota, the Gulf of Mexico and Lake Michigan all come together in the SW quarter of the state and provide some of the most beautiful scenery, most biologically diverse landscapes, and complex stories of human settlement and movement.

The highly interactive and engaging National Great Rivers Museum located at the Melvin Price Dam near Alton makes exploring these stories with grand-

children easier. The Army Corps of Engineers goes far beyond the lock and dam in developing a story that will captivate you for as much time as you can spare.

We watched kids of all ages enter the pilot house of the barge simulator and try to take the boat and barge through the bridges and locks of St. Louis. You will be in awe of the tug captains after you try.

The large map that shows in detail how the rivers come together is just what you need, short of an airplane, to see this area's rich and complex river systems. Large cutouts of historic people show how they traveled, explored, and lived along the river.

A model cliff brings the bluffs inside and illustrates where animals nest and live, while an aquarium helps you discover ancient species that still swim in these waters, connections that go all the way back to the dinosaurs.

You will learn about the river, but you will also find out about the value of water and that is a key concept for your grandchild.

Make sure you complete the variety of indoor exhibits before you take the tour of the locks. It will help give you a better perspective about the size and impact of this project.

Bonding and bridging:

There is no true separation between a river and a stream, a creek and a rivulet, but they all have in common the movement of water from one place to another. Philosophers loved to say you could never put your foot in the same river twice. This constant changing, the movement or energy are all things you can share with your grandchildren. It is the easiest of all science. Just put a stick in the water and watch it float, bring a toy boat and send it downstream or cast a fly for trout.

A river is a dynamic system with life forms in the rapids and pools. Explore and learn about rivers. Some of us find them the most significant of all geologic forms.

A word to the wise:

You can spend a lifetime exploring Illinois' big three rivers. The Illinois is 274 miles long—all in Illinois. Refuges along the Illinois include Chatauqua, Meredosia, Emiquon, and the Cameron/Billsbach. The Mississippi River Fish and Wildlife Area (MRA) is comprised of 24,386 acres and includes 15 wildlife management areas and 11 public access areas scattered along 75 miles of the Mississippi and Illinois rivers. There are 585 miles of paths and roadways that follow the 550 miles of Mississippi River that form the western border of Illinois. On the south end of the state the Ohio River completes its journey from Pennsylvania to the Mississippi and can be explored on the 188 miles of Illinois Ohio River Byway. On the east side of the state 200 miles of the border is created by the Wabasha River. State parks and unique cities make up this wonderful combination of travel adventures.

Age of grandchild: All

Best season: Summer and fall

Contact: National Great Rivers Museum, Melvin Price Locks and Dam, #1 Lock and Dam Way, East Alton, IL • (877) 462-6979
http://www.mvs.usace.army.mil/Rivers/museum.html
http://www.greatriverroad.com/Cities/EAlton/riverMuseum.htm

Also check out:

National Mississippi River Museum and Aquarium, Dubuque, IA; (563) 557-9545; www.mississippirivermuseum.com

Few things are more delightful than grandchildren fighting over your lap. DOUG LARSON

Lewis and Clark State Historic Site

When we talk about the Lewis and Clark Expedition of 1804/1805, we naturally think about the lands west of the Mississippi River and all the magnificent adventures they had during their 28 month odyssey. But few people know that the expedition made preparations and gathered information at a place called Camp River Dubois, at the confluence of the Mississippi and Missouri rivers.

The Lewis and Clark State Historic Site was built in a place thought to be close to the original winter camp of 1803 where William Clark and his men of the Detachment spent five months preparing the provisions for their upcoming journey.

The Visitor Center opened with the intention of telling the Illinois portion of this epic tale. The building is filled with beautiful wall murals that include quotes from the journals of various expedition members. In their own words, we can sense both their excitement and anxiety. Other displays show clothing of that time, items used in daily life, and a section that illustrates the rigors of a military lifestyle.

The most impressive part of this exhibit is the 55' replica of the keel-boat used by the Corps. This includes a 30' mast, which means that the room had to have a high peaked ceiling. With lots of windows along one wall, the space feels airy and bright. On one side, you see the boat's complete exterior form. The other side is a cutaway view with a fascinating display of items that were stored on board. You quickly realize how challenging it would have been to organize all the items for such a long and unknown journey. At a nearby table you and your grandchild can try your hand at loading toy size replicas of the keel boat with small wooden blocks, attempting to balance the weight properly, so that the boat doesn't tilt off kilter. It's much harder than it looks.

There are furs and bones that can be touched, but much of the exhibit involves reading. An excellent 15 minute film in the Convergence Theater will give you both an auditory and visual sense of the expedition, tying the preparations of the camp with scenes that flash forward to events during the most difficult parts of the journey.

Bonding and bridging:

Imagine how much has changed since the time when half of the country was unexplored. Today almost every inch of our country is known—by satellite image, if not by human footprint and we can click on Google Earth to see all the terrain and details. Ask your grandchild to try to imagine what it would feel like to go into a completely unknown land. What will be their unexplored territories? Outer space? Or deep inner space—our own DNA and genetics? Share an adventure or risk you took at some point in your life. It doesn't have to be a journey to a faraway place. It could be a new job or city, or going away to college. These are adventures, too.

A word to the wise:

This Historical Site is best for grandchildren old enough to know a bit about the history of our country. There is a replica of the 1803 camp built by Clark and his men, mainly a place to walk through unless you are there for one of the special events that take place throughout the year, when actors recreate the scenes of life in the camp. One event in January focuses on the lives of women in the early 1800s, often overlooked when a place focuses on the expeditions of men. In June, there is a special Kid's Day, when your grandchild can participate in rope making, military drills and flag folding, and learn to use a compass and telescope. If they complete all these activities they will receive a certificate declaring them a member of the Expedition.

Age of grandchild: 8 and up

Best season: Summer and fall

Contact: Lewis and Clark Sate Historic Site, One Lewis and Clark Trail, Hartford, IL 62048 • (618) 251-5811 • www.campdubois.com

Also check out:

Apple River Fort, Elizabeth; (815) 858-2028; www.appleriverfort.org

Annual Rendezvous at Fort de Chartes, Prairie du Rocher; (618) 284-7230; www.greatriverroad.com/stegen/randattract/fdcvous.htm

Fort de Chartes, Prairie du Rocher; (618) 284-7230; www.ftdechartres.com/

My grandkids believe I'm the oldest thing in the world. And after two or three hours with them, I believe it, too. GENE PERRET

Cahokia Mounds
State Historic Site

When we were growing up, we learned that Columbus discovered America, as if it were an uninhabited continent, but of course that is untrue, as Cahokia Mounds State Historic Site dramatically demonstrates. The people who lived in what is now southwest Illinois had a well developed culture, with as many as 20,000 people living in an agriculture-based society.

They are called the Mississippian culture because they lived along the great river, and their claim to fame is the immense mounds they built as part of their ceremonial life. The Monks Mound is the largest ever built in North America, covering 14 acres and rising 100 feet. It was the centerpiece of this community and the perch upon which the Chief ruled over the kingdom that spread out around him. Today, you can climb the 156 steps in the same place as the originals to the top of the mound and survey the land, as the royalty once did. As you and your grandchild stand there and slowly turn 360 degrees, try to picture what this land looked like in 900 A.D. Imagine no skyscrapers or refineries or freeway noise nearby. Imagine that the only sounds you hear are those of people working, playing and living in the grassy plain below. Or maybe you will hear the song of the meadowlark, and for a moment be a part of the past.

First visit the Interpretive Center, but before even entering, you see a huge pair of ornately cast bronze doors weighing approximately 800 pounds, covered with scenes of ravens flying over the Monks Mound. Once inside, check out the site model in the main lobby to get a sense of the layout of the original structures and mounds. Through the windows just beyond, you can see some of the grass covered mounds.

Be sure to view the award winning 15 minute orientation film, shown hourly, that will captivate young and old with the story of this land and the people who first lived here. The best part comes at the end of the film as the screen rises in front of you and a scene is revealed just beyond, as if you have just stepped back into time and are entering the daily lives of the people. The Interpretive Center has interactive exhibits and displays designed to help you visualize the people and their culture, before you venture outside to see and climb the actual mounds.

Bonding and bridging:

Children have a hard time grasping the scope of history. We grandparents seem as old as time to them, so trying to understand a place and culture that existed a millennium ago is really a challenge, but they also have vivid imaginations and the displays and lifelike representations of the people in the Interpretive Center help them to picture people like them living in a very different time. As you climb or walk around the mounds ask them what they think it would have felt like to be a child in this place and time. Ask them too what they think will remain of our culture in 1000 years, what they would want people to find that belonged to our time, to help define us.

A word to the wise:

Woodhenge is the replica of what were once five circular sun calendars. Each was created from red cedar posts, spaced in circles of varying diameters, used to mark the seasons and special ceremonial dates, based on the rising sun. You and your grandchildren can still experience this ancient practice at the Fall and Spring Equinoxes, as well as the Winter and Summer Solstices, organized by the site staff. It will mean getting up very early (depending on the season), but well worth the effort, when you can see how these ancient people created some very sophisticated processes for measuring time.

Age of grandchild: 7 and up

Best season: Summer

Contact: Cahokia Mounds, 30 Ramey Street, Collinsville, IL 62234
(618) 346-5160 • www.cahokiamounds.com

Also check out:

Dickson Mounds Museum, Lewistown; (309) 547-3721; www.museum.state.il.us/ismsites/dickson

Our children grow up so fast. Maybe grandchildren are God's way of giving us a second chance at participating in the miracle of life. UNKNOWN

103

Tunnel Hill State Trail

Bicycles provide carbon neutral exercise designed to fill the lungs with fresh oxygen, loosen up the leg muscles, provide scenery at a speed that can be enjoyed, and a social event that allows for sharing with a few people. What more can you possibly ask for in a good outdoor experience?

Well—you can ask for rolling terrain, lots of variety, and scenery that just doesn't stop. In short, you can ask for Tunnel Hill Bike Trail, one of Illinois'

best—maybe one of the top ten in the nation! And if you and your grandchildren are really into biking, this trail connects you to several trails including the River to River Trail; the Illinois southern route of the American Discovery Trail; the U.S. Bicycle Route 76 (part of the TransAmerica Bike Route); and the Trail of Tears National Historic Trail.

But what makes this so special for you and your grandchild? The 45 mile paved trail can be broken up to make eight easily accessible options, so you can choose the length that fits all of your needs. One section goes through the Cache River State Natural Area and provides lowland forests that feel like the swamps of the deep south. Here trees over 1000 years of age grow in dark waters.

The most famous section is the gradual slope that takes you over numerous narrow railroad trestles, each progressively higher above the valley bottoms and finally through the Tunnel that gives the trail its name. It reminds us of the days of railroading in the mid 1800s when tracks rather than freeways dominated our mobility. This railroad line also had the distinction of General Burnside—the man who gave us "sideburns" as one of the investors. The headquarters in Vienna is in a depot, reminiscent of this past.

Take an imaginary trip with us. Start on flat land and farm country before moving into the ancient cypress and tupelo forest, then hardwood forests and strands of prairie that lead to the rising lands of the Shawnee National Forest. Next the trail rises to its apex—300 feet above both ends and passes through an old dark railroad tunnel that gives the unit its name.

Bonding and bridging:

What is the light at the end of the tunnel? Maybe it is the reward we get for our efforts, the fact that physical and mental toughness finds unique rewards not open to those who sit passively and wait for the world to come to them.

What does it mean to use muscles instead of gasoline, to provide your own power rather than relying on a machine to do the work? Is it okay to be tired, to feel frustrated at times? Of course it is. We experience that regularly as adults. It is important for our grandchildren to work, to expend energy and to succeed.

A word to the wise:

There are outfitters who rent you bikes or give you shuttles. This is a good idea with kids because it keeps the trail new and the unknown is a good motivator. However, when you ride up and back you may find the second half of the trip to be anticlimactic and even boring for some. Avid riders among you will question this, but remember that the work our grandchildren do must be rewarded if we want them to continue to want to ride with us and explore.

Age of grandchild: 10 and up if you want them to be able to do a good solo ride.

Best season: Spring or fall

Contact: Tunnel Hill State Trail, PO Box 671, Vienna, IL 62995
(618) 658-2168 • http://dnr.state.il.us/lands/landmgt/parks/r5/tunnel.htm
http://illinois.sierraclub.org/shawnee/sites/s-tunnel_hill_bike_trail.htm

Also check out:

Grand Illinois Bike Trail; www.ipp.org/g-i-t.html

Illinois bike trails; www.dot.state.il.us/bikemap/trailist.htm

The charm of a woodland road lies not only in its beauty but in anticipation.
Around each bend may be a discovery, an adventure. Dale Rex Coman

Garden of the Gods

The most famous Garden of the Gods might be in Colorado Springs, but this underappreciated section of the Shawnee National Forest does not take a back seat to any natural garden of rock sculptures. This landscape is based on 320 million year old Pounds Sandstone of the Pennsylvanian Age, and a wilderness area adjacent to the small recreation area, comprising a total of 3,300 acres. Just be forewarned, you need to follow the map closely to find the Garden.

The sedimentary rocks are easy to walk on and will invite your grandchildren to climb and explore. Fortunately their grittiness reduces the potential for slipping, but there are some very steep drops and you will want to be very watchful of the young explorers.

The easy walk is only ¼ mile long from the parking lot, with handrails at times, and pavement all the way around. This is a high elevation walk among the round topped spires and provides magnificent looks in to the valley of the forest and ancient landscape and such famous formations as Honeycomb, Table Rock, Devil's Smokestack, Monkey Face and Camel. The colorful pattern of the sandstone features a unique iron banding and swirls called "Liesegange bands."

If you are more ambitious you can take the 5.5 mile trail in to the designated wilderness and discover "Anvil, Indian Pointe, Mushroom, and Big H" rocks. The longer trail is part of the famous River-to-River hiking trail and has lots of options for exploring and long distance hiking.

This raw rock landscape is unlike the glaciated central and northern sections of the state where topography is often unnoticeable. The continental glaciers stopped 15 miles north of this rocky area and the result is quite astounding. Geologists say that the rock formed almost one mile below the surface and then was brought up to the high elevation where it sits today, by a long fold in the rocks.

But more important in your experience is the sense of playfulness that the land creates. It is hard not to climb and play so you need to make an allowance for this and then end your visit by watching the sunset from one of the rocky overlooks.

Bonding and bridging:

If your grandchildren are old enough you might want to talk to them about the forces that shaped our earth.

All around are rocks of extraordinary ages, created by forces beyond anything we can assert as humans. Yet the final shaping of these landscapes was by the forces of sun, water, freezing, and melting.

Geologists are the people who read these stories and tell us where to find minerals and natural resources, where to build safely, and what the fossils and markings mean.

A word to the wise:

If you like to camp and want to give your grandchildren a longer opportunity to explore this little known area of Illinois beauty, a Pharaoh campground is open year-round with just 12 sites, picnic tables, fire pits, drinking water and pit toilets. Sometimes it is good to let a place grow on a child. They will have fun immediately in the hidden nooks and crevices, but with time they will discover more of the patterns, lines, and designs in the rocks, and they will begin to feel at home and come away with a long lasting impression.

Age of grandchild: 6 and up

Best season: Summer

Contact: Garden of the Gods, Hidden Springs Ranger District, Route 2, PO Box 4, Elizabethtown, IL 62931 • (618) 287-2201
www.backpackcamp.com/GardenOfTheGods.html
www.fs.fed.us/r9/forests/shawnee/recreation/wilderness

Also check out:

Shawnee National Forest;
www.fs.fed.us/r9/forests/shawnee/recreation/wilderness/

Hidden Springs Ranger Distric: Bay Creek, Burden Falls, Lusk Creek Wilderness; (618) 658-2214

Mississippi Bluffs Ranger District: Bald Knob, Clear Springs Wilderness: (618) 833-4511

Cypress Creek National Wildlife Refuge

Southern Illinois is nothing like its northern counterpart. It includes the remnant mountains of the Ozarks and cypress knees in the dark waters of the Cache River. This unique river runs parallel to the more famous Ohio, but unlike the Ohio, it does not carry the flow of the eastern states to the Mississippi River. While running east to west it actually gives the state the flavor of the southern waterways with swamps, cypress, and the maze of inundated lands.

It remains an important waterway for migrants, natural communities and recreationists who enjoy the beauty and seclusion of wild places.

The wet forests with 1000 year old cypress are living history books. They were growing when Leif Ericsson encountered the continent, and they were forests when Christopher Columbus landed in the West Indies.

Now they are a relic forest, an ancient landscape that extends beyond our memories into the historic past when the glaciers still stood in the Canadian wilderness. Important to us today, they are accessible because they have been protected in the Shawnee National Forest, the Cache River Natural Area, and in Cypress Creek National Wildlife Refuge.

The area offers waters for canoeing, boardwalks for hiking, wild lands for bird watching, and escape from the pressures of civilization. Here east meets west and north meets south. But more importantly this is a place for you to be with your grandchildren on the boardwalks or in a canoe, and have the world of nature surround you in a physical and psychological escape.

There are 18 miles of hiking trails in the natural area, as well as 6 miles of paddling. The Wildlife Refuge includes a wonderful Visitor Center where you can learn both the human and the natural history. The graphics in their displays are dynamic and there is a kids corner for the grandchildren to explore.

Bonding and bridging:

This is a good place for canoeing, quiet paddling and lots of surprises. If your grandchildren enjoying seeing new birds, if they like being in a landscape like the Lord of the Rings, or the land of dinosaurs, they will enjoy this paddle. Knees from cypress trees are sculptures in the water and resemble the landscape of fantasy novels. Brilliant warblers seem to appear out of the dark shadows.

The noise of civilization is replaced by the song of the land. You can talk about the long history of nature compared to the relatively short span of human existence. How have we come to be separated from the natural world?

A word to the wise:

The Barkhausen (Cache River) Visitor Center located on route 37 south of Whitehill is an excellent place to start your exploration. You can get maps and information while your grandchildren explore the wonderful exhibits. You can start planning your hikes and paddles, or begin your bird watching. The building is surrounded by a significant international wetland, a landscape recognized as a unique place for both plants and animals.

Age of grandchild: 8 and up

Best season: Spring, summer and fall

Contact:

Cache River State Natural Area, 930 Sunflower Lane, Belknap, IL 62908 (618) 634-9678 • http://dnr.state.il.us/lands/landmgt/parks/r5/cachervr.htm

Cypress Creek National Wildlife Refuge, 0137 Rustic Campus Drive, Ullin, IL 62992 • (618) 634-2231 • www.fws.gov/midwest/cypresscreek

Also check out:

Prairie Ridge State Natural Area; http://dnr.state.il.us/ORC/prairieridge/index.htm

Shawnee Forest—Heron Pond in the Cache River Natural Area, southern Illinois; www.umsl.edu/~loiselleb/Biol440/Shawnee/Index.html

Seeking Superman

Since time immemorial, humans have created superhuman heroes. It seems to be a deeply embedded psychological need in our species to imagine beings who are like us, only much better in body and spirit. How many of us have worn a cape—maybe it was just red fabric with our pajamas or a towel pinned to our shirt, but in our minds we were able to leave the confines of the earth and soar with the birds to do things invented in our day dreams.

Superman first appeared in the mid-30s when an American writer and a Canadian artist created a bald-headed villain. But the average Joe did not identify with him, so the creators changed a man into the Superman of the 1938 Action Comics #1. So began a reign of glory that continues to this day. He is the superhero that every child can name.

In what is now known as the "Golden Age of television," the 1950s, Superman came into our living rooms and his fame and familiarity continued to grow. In the classic scenario of small town boy drawn to big city lights, the young Clark Kent goes to a place called Metropolis—a modern beehive of economic growth and energy. The creators modeled it after Toronto, a city of grand skyscrapers.

This Metropolis is home to just 7000 people and there are no skyscrapers, but since 1972 this little southern Illinois community has completely embraced the Superman mythology. In that year the town received the designation "Home of Superman" from both DC Comics and the State Legislature. Today there is a larger than life statue standing guard in front of the City Hall and just kitty corner is the Jim Hambrick Super Museum and Store.

In 1978, the town hosted its first Superman Celebration, which is held the second weekend of June. This is probably the best time to visit Metropolis with your grandchildren. There are appearances by actors and actresses who have starred in various films or TV shows related to the Superhero; a special costume contest for the kids; Comic Arts Gallery; an outdoor theater film festival; contests emphasizing feats of strength for the adults; a Super dog show; a Super auction; a Super Trek Bicycle tour; and one year, a Super Wedding for the "Hollywood Superman."

Bonding and bridging:

As adults living in the real world, we are too well aware of the dangers and villains that exist. Our grandkids unfortunately know about many of these same problems, but together we can work on finding "Truth, justice, and the American way." After we leave the Museum or the Celebration, we can talk about the real ways we can find the best qualities of the Man of Steel. Honesty, helping others, and playing by the rules are the virtues that Superman demonstrates. We need to let our grandchildren know they have the ability to be as great as Superman, even without his super powers.

A word to the wise:

The Superman Museum holds the largest collection of Superman memorabilia in the world and has been given the number one rating by AAA three times in a row as the best small town attraction! But when you first walk into the building you are immediately in the store, so it is probably best to establish some rules or spending guidelines before entering. The Museum is located in another section of the building. This is the personal collection of one man and includes all manner of memorabilia, knick knacks, photos, movie posters and costumes of the super hero. All of these thousands of items are packed together pretty tightly into the exhibit space. Those over ten, who are familiar with Superman's history, will get the most out of the exhibit.

Age of grandchild: 5 and up

Best season: Summer

Contact:

Metropolis Chamber, 607 Market Street, Metropolis, IL 62960
(800) 949-5740 or (618) 524-2714 • www.metropolischamber.com

Super Museum, 517 Market Street, Metropolis, IL 62960 • (618) 524-5518
• www.supermancelebration.net

Also check out:

Popeye Statue, Chester; www.chesterill.com

The Chester Gould Dick Tracy Museum, Woodstock; (815) 338-8281; www.chestergould.org

Woodstock; www.woodstock-il.com

If you don't know [your family's] history, then you don't know anything. You are a leaf that doesn't know it is part of a tree. MICHAEL CRICHTON

Fort Massac State Park

This state park, Illinois' first, covers 1450 acres, but most of the action and interest centers on the reconstructed Fort and Visitor Center. The history of the site makes you wish for a time lapsed film to see how many times the walls and structures rose and fell. The causes include: fire, wear and tear, neglect and disrepair, dismantling and salvage by local settlers, and earthquake.

Situated on the banks of the broad Ohio River, this attractive site saw various groups of people, starting with the early Native Americans, the Spanish (if you believe local legends), followed by the French, the British, and finally the Americans.

Lewis and Clark stopped by in 1803 looking for recruits, and a few years later the New Madrid earthquake shook and damaged the Fort. In the 1970s a replica (1794) fort was built, which fell into disrepair and was replaced by the current 1802 version, built in 2002.

Before venturing through the stockade walls and over the bridge that crosses the dry moat, stop in the Visitor Center where you can watch a short film that will give you a good introduction to the site and its history. Other exhibits in the building display the uniforms worn by soldiers of different eras and countries, and a large collection of arrowheads and various musket balls. Archaeological digs have been ongoing since the 1930s.

In the Fort itself, your grandchildren will delight in running from building to building (there are two soldiers' barracks and one officers' quarters) and into the three blockhouses on the corners of the Fort. You can walk through the buildings and hear the echo of time as your feet hit the plank floorboards and reverberate through the empty rooms. Even on warm days it's easy to imagine how cold it would have been in these fireplace heated buildings in those long ago winters. The grandkids will especially love climbing up into the blockhouses where they can peer out through the small square windows at the river, imagining themselves as soldiers on the lookout for enemies approaching by water. Be on guard though, because access is by a straight up and down ladder and little feet may need some help.

Bonding and bridging:

As grandparents we represent living history and when we take our grandchildren to a place like Fort Massac we can give the experience a human face and feeling. You can help them to picture the people who once lived, worked, laughed, fought and died within these walls. Look at the way the logs were cut to build the walls or stockade and ask them how long it would take to do this work using only hand tools. And what about the dry moat that surrounds the Fort? That would have been dug by hand. Once they can picture real people doing these things, history becomes more immediate and impressive.

A word to the wise:

Like many historic forts, this one hosts an annual Encampment on the third weekend of October. This is a time when the Fort suddenly comes alive with people dressed in period costumes selling food and wares of the times. It is a festive setting and nothing makes 'ancient' history more interesting and fun than real live people who know their history very well and enjoy sharing their knowledge with visitors. There will be music and the sound of cannons firing. Traditional craftspeople demonstrate pottery, leatherwork, lace making, blacksmithing, wool spinning, and herbal arts. It is an exciting autumn festival and one that attracts thousands of visitors each year. Smaller scale events happen every weekend throughout the year—check with the Park for details.

Age of grandchild: 3 and up

Best season: Summer and fall

Contact: Fort Massac State Park, 1308 East Fifth Street, Metropolis, IL 62970 • (618) 524-9321
http://dnr.state.il.us/lands/Education/interprt/frtmass.htm

Also check out:

Apple River Fort, Elizabeth; (815) 858-2028; www.appleriverfort.org

Annual Rendezvous at Fort de Chartes, Prairie du Rocher; (618) 284-7230; www.greatriverroad.com/stegen/randattract/fdcvous.htm

Fort de Chartes State Historic Site, Prairie du Rocher; (618) 284-7230; www.ftdechartres.com

My grandfather was a giant of a man . . . When he walked, the earth shook. When he laughed, the birds fell out of the trees. His hair caught fire from the sun. His eyes were patches of sky. ETH CLIFFORD, *THE REMEMBERING BOX*

Bald Eagles and the Rivers

Talk about icons—how about mixing the nation's symbol, the Bald Eagle, with the father of waters, the Mississippi! Add in the Illinois River and you have Bald Eagle paradise. Along the beautiful river bluffs and some of the state's most magnificent state parks, eagle watching is a sport that everyone can enjoy. Because the eagles are so large, all the grandchildren will be able to

find and enjoy them, especially in the winter when eagles leave frozen lakes and streams and move to the open waters and food on the Mississippi and Illinois rivers.

Eagles do not like to migrate, but they have to move when their food supply gets low. Adult eagles force the young out of their area, to go farther south, when food sources diminish. As the winter gets harsher the young keep moving farther and farther, leaving us with an abundance of magnificent adults with white tails and heads that contrast with their black body and wings.

At one time this national symbol was on the endangered species list. Now more than 3,000 winter on Illinois rivers. What a great success story it has been.

Bald Eagle days and events are scheduled at Havana, Meredosia, Quad Cities, Rock Island, Quincy, Union (Union County Refuge), Pere Marquette State Park, Alton, Old Chain of Rocks Bridge (Granite City), Henry (Lock and Dam), National Great Rivers Museum, The Nature Institute (Godfrey), Clarksville, and Utica (Starved Rock State Park). All have eagle watching opportunities, eagle programs and guided observations. These are great because the kids will see eagles both close up and in their natural habitat and there are lots of experts to help you make this a memorable experience.

Bald Eagle days are not the only time to see the birds, but winter is definitely the best time. Try to view in the early morning (which is not that early in winter) because they are more active and feeding. Seeing them on the trees is great, but watching them soar and dive is much more dramatic. You might also see them eating carrion along any of the roads. Take your time, make good observations and make sure your grandchildren get as good a view as you do.

Bonding and bridging:

How do we save a species? There is no better lesson to teach our grandchildren than they can really make a difference in the world. The recovery of the bald eagle is one of the great stories of our time. It began with a woman named Rachel Carson, a scientist and chemist, who realized that when we were poisoning the mosquitoes with DDT, we were in fact spreading lethal chemicals to a far broader audience. Animals that ate insects accumulated this poison in their flesh—birds, fish, mammals. The top predators like eagles, peregrine falcons and osprey accumulated the most, and began to decline in numbers. When people learned what was happening, they spoke up, and the Endangered Species Act became law. This outlawed the indiscriminate use of poisons. This was a legacy to our grandchildren and they need to know that they are responsible for the actions that will affect future generations.

A word to the wise:

Combine an Eagle Days event with a visit to one of the parks or museums. Mix some trail time with your observations and go inside to view exhibits for part of the day if it is too cold. Keep some hot cocoa or apple juice in a thermos bottle and bring along some healthy snacks. Keep the energy reserves high in the cold and you will all have an excellent time.

Age of grandchild: 7 and up

Best season: Winter

Also check out:

Bald Eagle Watching; www.illinoisraptorcenter.org/eaglewatch.html

Illinois Raptor Center, Decatur; (217) 963-6909; www.illinoisraptorcenter.org

Great River Road events; www.greatriverroad.com/Eagles/eagleCover.htm

Illinois Tourism listings; www.enjoyillinois.com/features/eaglewatching.aspx

Canoeing

How did the first tourists travel the state? By canoe. Sure, some chose to walk the prairies, but it was the rivers and lakes that really got the early visitors around. People like Joliet, Marquette, DeSoto and other famous travelers knew a good thing when they saw it, and, thanks to the kindness of American Indians, they quickly learned the best way to glide up and down the rivers.

Today exploring waterways is still a great way to relax, learn, and get healthy exercise. It requires some skill, so don't take your grandchild out if you have not canoed before. Too many first-time paddlers go swimming unintentionally, and that is not how you want to have your grandchild learn about this marvelous sport.

We may not have a Boundary Waters Canoe Area in Illinois, but there is still wilderness paddling. The Cache River in southern Illinois is a world-class paddling adventure, without whitewater. In the Cache River Reserve there are magnificent, large old growth Bald Cypress (1000 years old!) and Tupelos—trees that are not only large, but exotic. Knees in black water and conifers that shed their leaves annually provide a mysterious setting even without the birds, reptiles and frogs, flowers and other species that we can't find anywhere else in the state.

The I&M Canal provides a different experience; here nature has reclaimed the manmade waterway and softened the impact of the canal structures. This leisurely paddle can be combined with bicycling for a perfect shuttle opportunity: paddling works the upper body and pedaling the lower.

The Kankakee, besides having a wonderful name, offers outfitters to provide you with canoe equipment and shuttles. Considered one of the state's cleanest rivers, the Kankakee is a perfect place to combine paddling and swimming. The Rock River south of Oregon is a great autumn paddle, with majestic colors.

No matter which river you take—the Vermilion, Fox, DuPage, Illinois, or the back waters of the Mississippi—canoeing is the perfect activity for conversation and contemplation.

Bonding and bridging:

In an age when everything has a motor and goes fast, grandparents can go a little slower. We can help children understand that slowing down is really experiencing more. The river meanders to slow down the flow of water to the ocean.

We paddle not to get somewhere, but to be somewhere, to notice the sun, the breeze, the strike of a fish on the line, the fresh scent of river air, the sound of swaying trees brushing branches against one another, or small birds calling out their territories.

A word to the wise:

If you feel up to it, a campout on a river trip is a very special opportunity to share and bond. A canoe allows you to bring more than if you were backpacking, and it puts you in remote sites where the quiet movement of the water becomes the background for setting up camp, making a meal, and sitting in front of a campfire.

A river makes you wonder where it's come from and where it's going. The waters gather from a distance and eventually move to the ocean and then back to a cloud filled with moisture, ready to rain and start the process all over again. To sit beside the river, toss sticks in and watch them go, is an invitation to speak of big dreams and the mysteries that fill the young mind.

Age of grandchild: 8 and up

Best season: Spring, summer and fall

Also check out:

Paddling places; http://www.paddling.net/places/IL/

Vermilion River; www.canoethevermilion.com

Canoe Trip Outfitters;
www.yellowbook.com/Category/canoe_trip_outfitters/Illinois/

Illinois Tourism; www.enjoyillinois.com

Illinois Paddling Council; www.illinoispaddling.org

Illinois Weather

As we write this, the region is in a heat wave, causing anguish and frustration. But what are we angry about and why do we continue to fight the weather? Surely we have to construct buildings to keep us cool, to help us withstand the forces of storms, but overall, weather is a gift of variety and new opportunities.

Grandparents can help grandchildren avoid weather phobia—glued to the Weather Channel and constantly too warm, too cold, too wet, too windy— by helping them to have fun in "bad weather". It is harder in the city when the only interaction with nature is getting to the car, the bus, the plane, the office, or the school. Then weather is a nuisance, but does it help to complain about the weather? Shouldn't we get the most out of all our experiences?

Think back to your childhood. Did you always want to come in when it rained? Did you want to be inside because it was cold or snowy? We know our grandchildren would like to be out playing and if that is not possible they still want a fun day. So set aside some special activities for the most challenging weather.

Getting dirty is normal and not something to avoid. Do you remember running out in the rain, jumping in puddles, making mud pies? Many of these things don't happen now. Not because the kids wouldn't enjoy them, but because it is easier to bring the children inside. Small children think an umbrella is fun and they need to walk with you in the rain. A big tree canopy is another form of umbrella and it is amazing to see how much rain the leaves catch. Watch how the rain moves from leaf to leaf.

Snowmen, snow forts, and snowballs can be fun. It is simple to put a piece of black felt on a board, let it get cold, then catch snow flakes that you can look at with a magnifying glass.

If it is really too bad to be out, have some games and puzzles set aside. Changing our attitude about "bad weather" can give us all many more good days in our lives.

Bonding and bridging:

Almost everyone complains about weather. But what is weather? Of all the events in our world, this is one thing that your grandchildren can observe and study wherever they are.

Tell your grandchildren about the big storms you have seen. Tell them about John Muir, the great naturalist, who would tie himself to tree tops, in order to feel the wind. Talk about a cold day you've experienced, and how that would be a warm day to a polar explorer or an Inuit. How hot is it for people on the equator and in the rainforest? Whatever the weather, each day is a new experience to understand and enjoy.

A word to the wise:

We do not want to belittle extreme weather. It is important to dress correctly and we need to know about sunscreen, windbreakers, rain jackets, and warm winter clothing. Think of how much easier it is to use these things if the child understands why. Weather has only three ingredients—wind, temperature, and moisture—but how much variety those three elements can create!

Age of grandchild: 5 and up

Best season: All

Also check out:

Illinois weather; www.weathercentral.com/weather/us/states/IL/

Central Illinois weather from NOAA; www.crh.noaa.gov/ilx/

Illinois climate records; www.sws.uiuc.edu/atmos/statecli/index.htm

City Parks

We are fortunate that there have been people with the foresight to realize that putting land into public ownership is for the public benefit and we can take advantage of this wonderful sense of community and nature by walking, playing, and exploring the natural landscapes.

There are two types of parks found in the city. One is the recreational park designed with ball diamonds, picnic tables, and recreational options in organized play and sports. These are great assets and places to engage in organized play and sports. Luckily, cities like Springfield, Bloomington, Peoria, and Rockford have wonderful city parks, just as Chicago does, so you do not have to travel long distances to find your location.

The second type of park is the one that may have the most value to the grandparents, grandchildren and society. These are parks that allow the thread of wildness to interlace with our community development. These are green connections to the natural world, a reminder of what the earth is like without buildings and development. They are simple places where play is dictated by imagination and inspiration.

Think of the park as a blank palette. You approach it with your grandchildren with a few throw toys, a little art paper and crayons, a blanket, some snacks, and most of all, your creativity. The beauty of an open park is in the endless variations on the theme of play and discovery. Shuffling through leaves might lead to piling up the leaves and crawling in or flopping on them. Pebbles get thrown in the water, twigs float.

It is a place for "hide and seek," in a world ready for imagination and creativity. Your job is to be there, to be ready to respond and to encourage. There is no single thing you do here other than give the experience time. Your grandchildren will see the possibilities. They will engage and you need to join in.

Chase the butterflies, listen to the birds, catch raindrops on your tongue, put paper on the bark of the trees and use crayons to rub on the paper to catch the texture and design.

Then sit on the blanket or at the picnic table to have refreshments and talk about your day.

Bonding and bridging:

Our local parks connect grandparents who enjoy the fresh air and sunshine with grandchildren who engage in play and imagination. The playground equipment nowadays is often elaborate and multi-level, so that kids can spend hours creating imaginary places and settings. These times of innocent play and sharing also help develop a sense of place. Our communities are places where we work and live, but in addition, a healthy community is one where open and green space has been set aside to provide its citizens with a place to rejuvenate and retreat from the noise and distractions of city life. We have city parks because we know that these places are at least as valuable as a mall, or a stadium. That is an understanding we hope future generations will continue to share and we can help promote it early in life.

A word to the wise:

Fill your backpack with a few simple things that can help your grandchild collect art to bring home.

1. Bring a notebook and crayons (just a few). You can always draw pictures, but, instead, place the paper over the bark of a tree or over a leave and rub the crayon over it to capture an image and texture.

2. Place leaves you like in the notebook. Write any note, poem, or thoughts about the leaf. When it dries, cover it with clear contact paper. Cut around the finished piece with a little margin around the edge. Use string to make a mobile.

3. Bring a few corks in case there is a stream—nothing better than seeing these little corks drift with the current. Decorate them and then collect them afterward.

4. Magnifying glasses aren't just for Sherlock Holmes!

5. Binoculars can work for older children, but young children will need practice to see the object they are looking for.

6. A digital camera for older children can be a good focus for their interest.

Age of grandchild: All

Best season: All

Cooking Together

Cooking with your grandchildren will add memories of all sorts in a very positive way. Depending upon their age you can let them use a cookie cutter and decorate your creations, or you can engage them in measuring, mixing, baking, and, of course, eating.

Be prepared, as you search out appropriate recipes, to do the majority of work. If they get bored and wander off, don't force them back. They will come back for the tasting. Be patient and let them get intrigued. Success comes from following some simple rules.

Choose a recipe that your grandchild will like. This should be a very simple recipe to start with, but in one case, we chose complex and challenging recipes to teach a teenager who really wanted to learn. She was motivated by the challenge.

Put an apron on everyone (we know that aprons are getting harder to find) and wash hands. Good hygiene is a good lesson and cleanliness might be tough to achieve, but keep it in mind.

Set out the ingredients ahead of time. When you invite them to cook with you, the last thing you want to do is make them wait while you sort out your cupboards. Set up stations that keep the children away from sharp knives and hot pans. There will be three "stations"—one for mixing ingredients, the oven or stove for cooking them, and another spot for decorating or serving the results. Use a stool if necessary, so that they are even with the counter and not stretching. Help them measure, but do it over a separate bowl so that extra ingredients do not fall into your final product.

For younger children, decorating is the most fun, although eating ranks very high. In fact, dough may start disappearing before it gets to the oven. How can you beat an activity that is hands-on, has great smells, looks good, and tastes great?

Bonding and bridging:

In our research we came upon a significant state-ment—'build kids not cookies'. This is about sharing and creating. They are learning where food comes from, they are doing something that has a great outcome, and they are beginners. Do not rush, do not use the phone, or do other distracting activ-ities. This is not a time for multi-tasking, but a time for concentration.

When the final products are done, especially with baked goods, there is the lesson of delayed gratification while you wait for your creation to cool before you eat it. Think of some things you can do during this time.

You might set a nice place at the table and create a fun drink while you wait.

A word to the wise:

A good beginning exercise for young kids is making play dough. All you need is 7–8 cups of flour, 3 cups of salt, 3 tablespoons of cream of tartar, ¼ cup of vegetable oil, 4 cups of hot water, and some food coloring. Mix the first three, add oil and water, and knead. Break up the dough in to smaller units so you can make different colors when you knead.

Parcel out the work! Two year olds can scrub and tear, three year olds can mix and pour, and 4–5 year olds can measure and beat.

Age of grandchild: 3 and up

Best season: Winter

Also check out:

Better Homes and Gardens Children's Favorites; www.bhg.com/recipes/childrens-favorites

The Prepared Pantry; www.preparedpantry.com/bakingwithkidsinfopage.htm

National Network for Child Care; www.nncc.org/Curriculum/fc46_cook.kids.html

Young Chefs Academy; www.youngchefsacademy.com

State Parks

Illinois has 48 state parks, plus wildlife areas, forests, and natural areas for you to explore. Each has a unique place and history, but they all belong to the people of Illinois, living museums of natural history, places of recreation, camping, hiking and boating.

Parks give you access to the wild lands that few people could afford to acquire for themselves and they dot the state with refuges for wildlife and plants.

Some locations deserve special visits, but all the state parks form a connection for grandparents and grandchildren to the land that is different from city parks and zoos. Walking, picnicking, and exploring have freedom inherent in the experience that really lets each person connect with place, experience, and landscape.

Sometimes Illinois doesn't get its due credit as a "natural" state, but look at the long Mississippi river shoreline, with Palisade and Pere Marquette parks, and Starved Rock on the Illinois River with the bluffs, forests, eagles, mollusks, migrating birds, fur bearers and Indian encampments. Or the short stretch of the Ohio with parks like Cave in the Rocks, and the shoreline on Lake Michigan with Illinois Beach. Each is unique in both plant life and recreational opportunities.

You can visit the great moraines from the glacial ice ages and the rugged, unglaciated land in the southern tip with its hills and rocky ridges. A prairie links Illinois with the Great Plains, hardwood forests connect you with the land from Wisconsin to the Gulf. Bogs and natural areas make you feel like you are in Alaska or northern Minnesota, and the Illinois River cuts a swath of floodplain forests through the heart of the farm land.

In the southern part of the state City of Giants has great rock formations and hidden nooks waiting to be discovered. Nearby is Fern Clyffe with its beautiful flora hidden in the rich, moist soils of the Shawnee Hills. You can also choose to swim, boat and fish at Dixon Springs, Lake Murphysboro or Ramsey Lake.

The challenge is to visit each park and find the unique characteristics that set it apart from all the others.

Bonding and bridging:

What is better than a new discovery? It does not have to be earth shattering, just something that you have never seen before.

Together on a hike, on a picnic or just watching the clouds float by, let your mind absorb the smells, sights, and sounds. Look for something you've never seen before; something new to both of you and when you find it, put it in a journal, take a photograph, draw a picture.

Capture that image as a treasure that you share forever. It will be a—"do you remember when . . ." time, and we can never have too many of those.

A word to the wise:

Pere Marquette State Park is famous for bald eagles during the winter and exquisite fall colors. The park was named for Father Jacques Marquette, a French missionary who landed here in 1673.

Chain O'Lakes State Park contains part of three natural lakes—Grass, Marie and Nippersink—and the Fox River that connects to another seven lakes—Bluff, Fox, Pistakee, Channel, Petite, Catherine and Redhead—which make up the chain.

Mississippi Palisades State Park, named for the line of lofty, steep cliffs along the river, has caves and sinkholes in this land of erosion-carved rock formations.

Starved Rock State Park contains fascinating rock formations in the 425 million years old St. Peter sandstone. The Illinois River Valley in the Starved Rock area is a dramatic contrast to the surrounding flatland.

Fern Clyffe State Park in the Shawnee Hills is a beautiful combination of hills, fishing lake, beautiful spring flowers, and rocky slopes covered with ferns and mosses.

Age of grandchild: All

Best season: All

Contact: Illinois Department of Natural Resources, Office of Land Management, One Natural Resources Way, Springfield, IL 62702 • (217) 782-6302 • dnr.parksadmin@illinois.gov • http://dnr.state.il.us/lands/landmgt/PARKS/index.htm

Grandparents are made in Heaven, born with the birth of their first grandchild. Gail Lumet Buckley

Fireworks

There is something exciting about fireworks that is hard to find in any other shared adventure with your grandchildren. Maybe it's the fact that you are actually telling them to stay up late, that you are taking them out in the dark, and that you are going to watch a sky display that is not only colorful, loud, and unusual, but something that would be illegal if you did it yourself.

While there are many places to view and even buy fireworks in Illinois, it is hard to beat the Navy Pier where they set off fireworks all summer long. No need to wait for July 4 on this festive dock, since there is a display every Wednesday and Saturday night!

Imagine the color of the carnival, the lights of the city, and the reflections on the lake, and you will know why this is the place to be. Of course, July 4 is still the number one pyrotechnic day and in Chicago that means going to Grant Park where the Taste of Chicago ends in a blaze of color.

The 4th of July celebrations are not limited to Chicago. Small town fireworks can be a wonderful way to see the true meaning of the national celebration. In Henry County in East Central Illinois you can enjoy the late morning parade in Hooppole and participate in their toad and frog jumping contest

(bring your own), get pork chops in Geneseo, catch the lighted night parade in Orion, and enjoy Prophetstown's "Best Fireworks in the Area." This is their claim; you can be the judge.

In some ways, this is an opportunity for grandparents to begin to remove some of the fear of dark that is so instilled in many of our children. A perfect summer evening, a blanket spread on the grass of the park, or near the lake, a pillow to put under your head and you are ready.

First there is the night sky and if you are lucky enough to be in a place where the stars are able to shine through, you can begin to find simple sky patches like the big dipper and the north star to help you wait; then when the show starts let them 'oooh' and 'ahhhh' along with you.

Bonding and bridging:

Fireworks have a fascinating place in our American psyche. They are both the overwhelming sensation of light and sound and a symbol. Talk about the connection between the Fourth of July and our national anthem. What is it that makes the fireworks so much a part of our nation's most important holiday? What is the connection between the lyrics of our national anthem and the most audacious part of our annual celebration? Here is a chance to talk about symbols, patriotism, and celebration. This is a story that will take time to understand, but observing the fireworks is a time to explore additional meaning.

A word to the wise:

Remember, children are not used to being up this late and they do not know how dangerous fireworks can be. Give them some safety tips in a positive environment.

Another option is to take a boat out from the Pier and let your grandchildren watch the event from the water. For something really different, there is the Rockford display over the river, purported to be the largest display in the state, preceded by a motorcycle and a Studebaker parade!

Age of grandchild: 3 and up

Best season: Summer

Also check out:

Fireworks Fun; www.fireworksfun.com/illinois-fireworks.asp

Happy Birthday America; www.usacitylink.com/usa

Springfield Air Rendezvous, Springfield; (217) 789-4400; www.springfield-il.com/airshow

Amish Country fireworks, Arthur; www.illinoisamishcountry.com/events/fireworks

Taste of Chicago; www.tasteofchicago.us

Navy Pier, Chicago; (312) 595-PIER; www.navypier.com

Rockford; www.ci.rockford.il.us

How beautifully the leaves grow old. How full of light and color are their last days. John Burroughs

Kite Flying

If you are looking for a simple activity that connects wind, energy, flight—it is hard to beat a kite. If you are looking for something that is almost magic—build your own with string, ribbon, newspaper, and wood. Can you imagine those ingredients taking you into the atmosphere? How do you shape the kite? Why a tail? Do you run with the wind, against or across? These have been pondered and experimented with since 1000 BC in China and we still work with the same basic elements to make a sailboat move, support a parasail or a hang glider.

Marco Polo brought kites from China to the western world and the western world used them in practical ways. Alexander Wilson flew thermometers on his kites, Archbold flew anemometers, and Benjamin Franklin survived a really dumb experiment—flying a kite in a lightning storm. Ships released kites if they were in danger and hoped there would be a rescue as a result, and kites in life rafts helped rescuers spot the drifting boats.

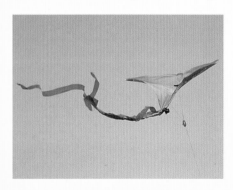

I still have memories of a clear sunny day with gusty winds on a hill when I was a child. There was a wonderful clear field of grass, surrounded by a boulevard of oak trees. My parents and grandparents had purchased a box kite, one of the first purchased kites I'd ever had. We assembled it and the excitement grew. The breeze blew. I ran and ran and ran, and it seemed as if I was destined to have the only earthbound kite in the park, but then it took flight and we were playing out the string, watching it rise, feeling the pull of the wind. We were tethered to flight and it was exhilarating, until finally it was time to reel it in. The kite fought the command to return to the ground and as a last vestige of independence it found an oak tree. My grandfather and my father both thought that they could get it down. Now I wonder—is my dad's shoe still lodged in that oak branch?

There is no better place for kite flying than on the shore of Lake Michigan, and Chicago's parks are an excellent place for catching the wind, but definitely not the only place in Illinois. Salem has an annual Kite Flying contest, as does the Chicago Botanic Garden in Glencoe.

Bonding and bridging:

What is more pleasurable and simple than running across a grass field, string in hand, kite taking flight? This is the essence of shared experience. It is not the money we spend, the glitz and glamour that connect us with our grandchildren, but rather the quiet sharing of discovery. How did we human beings learn to control the wind and rise to the sky? Does the kite teach us anything about flight? How perfect an opportunity to talk about Wilbur and Orville Wright, da Vinci, and all the dreamers of flight who have led us to our modern planes and rockets. The kite is our thread to the sky. It was Ben Franklin's means to learn about electricity; maybe it is your means to explore your dreams about the universe.

A word to the wise:

We used to think of kites as summer recreation, but the extreme skiers and snowboarders have found that they can harness themselves to modified kites and be pulled, often airborne, across the frozen lakes. This is a combination of two colorful sports you can watch in Madison, Chequamegon Bay, and on other lakes. Have fun and watch these skiers catch the wind. Someday it might be your grandchild out there.

Age of grandchild: 3 and up

Best season: Spring and fall

Also check out:

Kite Flying Contest, Salem;
www.salemil.us/Pages/SalemIL_Rec/programs/flykites

ChicagoKite, Chicago; (773) 467-1428;
www.chicagokite.com/ilstwidkifly.html

Kite Festival, DeKalb; (877) DEKALB1; www.dekalbareacvb.com;

Perry Farm Kite Festival, Bourbonnais; (815) 933-9905;
www.btpd.org/1Events_PerryFarmKiteFestival.htm

Forget not that the earth delights to feel your bare feet, and the winds long to play with your hair. KAHLIL GIBRAN

Grandparents Day

Grandparents are special; we can play an important part in the raising of healthy grandchildren and because of that we deserve a Day! But our Day ranks far below Mother's Day and Father's Day. Maybe that is because we have not stepped forward to get the recognition we need. So we say—step up, make this Sunday after Labor Day special and ask that on this day, you can spend quality time with your grandchild.

This national day was first established in 1973 in West Virginia through the efforts of Marian McQuade, a mother of 15 from West Virginia who was as dedicated to the care of senior citizens as she was to children. She formed the Forget-Me-Not Ambassadors, to make sure that senior homes were visited regularly. In 1978, President Jimmy Carter recognized this effort and named a national day of commemoration.

President Carter at the signing of the new legislation said, "Whether they are our own or surrogate grandparents, who fill some of the gaps in our mobile society, our senior generation also provides our society a link to our national heritage and traditions."

The first Sunday after Labor Day, Grandparents Day may be overlooked in the transition to the school year, autumn and family schedules. But don't allow it to be forgotten. Instead, make it a day that brings grandchildren in to honor the grandparents lives. Your children can help make this happen, but it can be a success if you do the planning, too.

The day is not about going somewhere for outside entertainment. Have a cake, have a celebration, but concentrate on the things that made your childhood special. Play some of the old board games. Make a rocket ship out of a cardboard box (I bet you can remember doing that); thread spools attached to the box for controls, crayon scenes for windows. Gather everyone around and tell a story about your childhood and make this a day of photo albums.

This day is about you and for you. Make your life and your love the focus for this special time.

Bonding and bridging:

In this world, it can be hard for people to show their true feelings. Saying, "I love you," almost seems taboo. Why that is, I do not know. But Grandparents Day is a good time to remember that it's okay to let your family members know they are loved.

We were lucky. The night my father died we talked on the phone and I said 'I love you dad'. He was gone three hours later. The week our son, Matthew, died I told him I loved him. It was our last conversation. Waiting to say "I love you" can leave you empty. Express yourself when you can. You will never regret that you reached out to someone special.

A word to the wise:

Choose a special activity like those described in this book and repeat it each year. Traditions are built upon repetition, like Kate's grandmother making chicken and mashed potatoes every Sunday night, or Mike's grandmother making blackberry pie every July. Later we are rewarded by memories that are triggered by an old car, a special taste, the color of a favorite sweater, the smell of aftershave or perfume. On this day of all days, provide your grandchild with the things that will bring back memories decades later.

Age of grandchild: All

Best season: First Sunday after Labor Day

Also check out:

For old time candy, try:
  www.oldtimecandy.com
  www.hometownfavorites.com
  www.sweetnostalgia.com

See if one of them might have the assortment that brings back memories to your tastebuds and shares a bit of your childhood with your grandchildren. We were flooded with nostalgia when we opened our first box and gave away numerous boxes to friends for Valentine's day, for the fun of sharing memories.

If a child is to keep alive his inborn sense of wonder, he needs the companionship of at least one adult who can share it, rediscovering with him the joy, excitement and mystery of the world we live in. RACHEL CARSON

Picnicking

"Let's have a picnic". Such a simple phrase, but it had so much meaning when I was growing up. It meant we were going to a park where I could explore, and it probably meant that we would be meeting my grandparents.

The picnic always meant packing food and dishes in a basket, bringing the charcoal, and a tablecloth. Why is a picnic tablecloth always a red check? There would be a cooler for cold dishes and some soda pop. Then my grandmother

would come with a hot dish wrapped in a dish towel. She had it wrapped almost like a turban—I still don't know how she did it, but even more surprisingly, that towel somehow managed to keep the dish and its contents hot for fifty miles!

This was a wonderful setting. We would greet, bring out the food and sit and eat in fresh air, surrounded by green plants and open space. It was a paradise of opportunity for an inner city boy. After the food was leisurely consumed, it would be time to sit in a folding chair, or go for a short walk. Grandpa would usually accompany me on this stroll—"letting the food settle" was the code phrase for it.

Picnicking is one of the real simple pleasures that may get overlooked in this world of fast food, fast service, and fast pace, but perhaps it is the antidote that is most needed. Spill something? So what? Get food on your clothing—no big deal. Leave the hang-ups from home at home. Relax. Eat with you fingers! Crack open the watermelon and spit the seeds.

Don't bring fast foods in their takeout bag to a picnic. A real picnic involves preparation and anticipation. It's a meal, time to roam, time to talk, maybe a swim, and then a revisit to the leftovers.

Most city and state parks have picnic areas that will meet your needs, but it is worth searching out special ones too. For example, Firefly Picnic Grounds in the Morton Arboretum not only is beautiful, but connects to the maze and the children's garden. Or you could attend a picnic event like the Popeye Picnic in Chester.

Bonding and bridging:

The old adage is that 'the way to a man's heart is through his stomach', but perhaps we have to include just about everyone and especially our grandchildren. The picnic is all about setting and comfort foods.

Let the grandchild help with the planning and the preparation. See what makes it perfect for them and why. What is it that we like about certain foods? Beans in a brown crock will always be good, but a picnic needs watermelon as the coup de grace to make it perfect.

A word to the wise:

Even the word picnic is unusual—it first was known as "pique-nique" in France and later—in the 1800s as picnic in England. Originally it was a gathering (potluck) like the family reunions we used to go to each summer. In England, the Picnic Society formed for a short period. The group would gather with food from all the participants and no particular host. The German version is PICK-NICK. In 1989, the PanEuropean Picnic was a famous gathering and protest to reunify Germany.

Through all these versions a picnic remains a way to gather large groups without having to open your house or cook all the food. What an excellent idea.

Age of grandchild: All

Best season: Spring, summer and fall, but don't rule out a winter picnic.

Also check out:

Firefly Pond Picnic Area, Morton Arboretum, Chicago; www.chicagofun.com/mortonarboretum/index.html

State Parks; www.dnr.state.il.us/lands/landmgt/parks

Popeye Picnic, Chester; www.popeyepicnic.com/stories.shtml

Picnic food ideas: www.fabulousfoods.com/holidays/picnic/picnic.html

More picnic foods; www.cooks.com/rec/search?q=picnic

Hot Air Balloon Ride

With all the rockets and satellites in space, airplanes of all sizes and speeds, helicopters in war and patrolling the streets, the air does not seem as mystical as it did when Buck Rogers and Flash Gordon were discovering the strange civilizations and adventures of outer space or as organized and civilized as it was from the starship Enterprise. But the sight of a colorful balloon rising in the sky with a wicker basket full of people dangling below can still inspire imagination and desire for adventure.

Sometimes it is the return to simplicity that gives us the clearest path to imagination, and a hot air balloon cruising over farm fields, along the Illinois, Ohio or Mississippi rivers, riding above the tree tops and moving through the sky can be a wonderful inspiration.

Hot air balloons are really not quiet when you are in them, but the noise of the massive heaters can't take away the feeling of floating, and the sense that you are part of the wind— connected to the currents in the air. Like other air vehicles, balloons allow you to adjust the up and down elements, but, unlike others, not direction or distance. You really must commit to the ride and allow nature to decide the destination.

And what a way to learn science! The basic knowledge is that hot air rises and cold air falls. Hawks demonstrate this when they soar over a field, or along the bluffs of the Mississippi River. The sun warms the dark rocks or vegetation and air rises from the south facing slopes, but sinks in the rivers and over the lakes. Hot air balloons take advantage of, but do not rely on landforms for their heat; instead they use a burner under a balloon that is open and ready to trap heated air.

Now for the science: A cubic foot of air weighs about 28 grams (an ounce) and when it is heated it loses about seven grams of weight. That is the amount of weight that the cubic foot of heated air can lift, so if we think about how much weight 7 grams is, we know that it will not provide much aeronautical lift. The 1000 pounds of basket, heater, and people that fill the basket need close to 65,000 cubic feet of heated air to rise above the earth. That is why the balloon is so big and the basket so small! This is why they prefer to fly early in the morning when it takes less heat to get off the ground. Think of how much heat it would take for the balloon to rise on a hot summer afternoon.

Bonding and bridging:

Whatever aviation was in your youth, it could not compare with what the children of today see and watch. We remember the amazement of the Apollo missions and a man walking on the moon. Our parents remembered Lindbergh's flight to Paris and our grandparents were young when Orville Wright took his halting first flight. Our children will remember the Mars missions, the space station and the Hubble space telescope. What will our grandchildren observe?

A grandparent can help give perspective to the grandchild. And maybe we can get perspective on our grandchildren's view of their world.

A word to the wise:

Flight may have lost the fascination it deserves. Kids may start to think people are supposed to fly—they aren't. A hot air balloon is a step back to the basics. Just watching it inflate is a wonderful experience. So after the flight, fly a kite, play with helium balloons, learn about flight and kindle imagination. If you are fortunate you can find the old balsa wood gliders we played with.

Age of grandchild: 10 and up

Best season: Fall

Also check out:

Balloon Association of Greater Illinois; www.bagiballoon.org

P I Ball Balloons, Rock Island; (309) 787-0107

Ascension Ballooning Ltd, East Moline; (309) 792-3000

Yankee Spirit Balloon Flights, Manito; (309) 968-7170

Skycruiser Balloon Promotions, Lincoln; (217) 735-4433

Forest City Hot Air Balloon, Rockford; (815) 397-4901

Aerosport Management, Batavia; (630) 879-6733

Lake Michigan Beaches

There are many lakes in Illinois with good beaches, including many in state parks, but there is only one Great Lake, one cold and clear, with a horizon big enough to capture the curvature of the earth, and that is Lake Michigan.

Lake Michigan is the only Great Lake not shared with Canada. It is 307 miles north/south and 118 miles across making it the world's fifth largest lake. It is the focal point for Chicago and the suburbs and communities that extend north to Wisconsin.

In the summer it is a magnet from North Beach to Illinois Beach State Park. North Beach is one of 28 named beaches in the metropolitan area. This is the escape hatch when the summer heat index reaches in to the 80s, 90s, and 100s. Kids love to play in the water and build castles in the sand. North Beach has an international volleyball competition and is the center of the Chicago Air and Water Show, but all the beaches are popular and important parts of the summer landscape.

We can see the beauty in the sails, the magnificent ships, including an occasional square rigger, the allure of the lighthouses and the contrast between harbor and cityscape, but for our grandchildren it is the magic of sand and water! Think about it from their perspective: a sandbox without boards, a swimming pool without metal steps. This is as close to paradise as children can find.

In all our research and in all the states we visit, nothing draws our grandchildren like water. They want to wade in it, throw rocks in it, splash, sit, float boats, and build castles in the sand. Nothing more elaborate. Your job is to keep them safe and encourage their imagination. Get down and build a castle (or start it and let them take over). Bring just enough little toys to add interest, but concentrate on the imagination. They will see the other aspects of the beach when they are ready.

If we were to survey the grandchildren about our recommendations—we believe, the beach would be their fist pick.

Bonding and bridging:

Wade in the water and play in the sand. Play is how we develop motor skills, dexterity and problem solving. We play because it is fun, we learn because we are doing something that involves creating, experimenting, and sometimes failing. The hard part can be when they want to add something to our castle that we do not think will work or fit our design. Give it up. Let the project be for the children, not for the adult. If it is not perfect in adult eyes, so be it. The test is in the children's eyes. Leave the battery operated boats, cars at home. The beach is about simplicity. Add water, sand, and child—stir in creativity and give it time.

A word to the wise:

Sunscreen is essential. Do not let the cool breeze or cool water fool you. We know that sunburns when we are children can lead to skin cancer when we are older. Pick up sunscreen designed for children over six months with both UVA and UVB protection. SPF 15 is the minimum protection level, higher is better. Apply it thick and often. The recommendation is 30–45 minutes before going out and every two hours (more if there is a lot of swimming or perspiring).

Protective clothing helps, but clothes offer only partial protection. Try to go to the beach later so you limit the most intense exposure (10am–4pm). Clouds do not eliminate sun radiation. Eyes are also impacted by sunlight so let your kids be cool and get some shades! And finally, insect repellent can reduce the effectiveness of sunscreen.

Age of grandchild: 3 and up

Best season: Summer

Contact:

Illinois Beach State Park, Lake Front, Zion, IL 60099 • (847) 662-4811
http://dnr.state.il.us/lands/landmgt/parks/r2/ILbeach.htm

Chicago beaches; Chicago Park District • (312) 742-PLAY
www.chicagoparkdistrict.com/resources/beaches

Also check out:

Wolf Creek State Park; www.stateparks.com/wolf_creek.html

Illinois State Parks; www.illinoisparksandrecreation.com/links/index.htm

It's funny what happens when you become a grandparent. You start to act all goofy and do things you never thought you'd do. It's terrific. MIKE KRZYZEWSKI

Fishing

A translucent line, a hook, a sinker, a worm, and a pole: what a list of ingredients for something that could change a life. Fishing is one of the most basic sports in the world and also one of the most popular. If there is water around, fishing is part of the scene. Of course it is a multi-billion dollar industry, but fun is not based on what you spent, but rather what you caught, and a sunny nibbling at the bait is a terrible tease, just as a small bass is an explosion of energy and excitement.

Grandparents need to keep the activity simple. You do not need massive boats and engines, depth finders and tackle boxes that need block and tackle to lift. Just get the basics and take your grandchild to the lake or the river. It is excitement and anticipation. Maybe it is even magic. Drop a worm in, pull a fish out.

It is the panfish you want to start on. They are simple, they are abundant in the right places and your grandchild can experience success in a hurry. If you make them work for the big one, you are likely to see the excitement replaced with boredom. Make the first fishing trip about their excitement, not the record lunker. Try for the bluegill which one fishing expert says is ounce for ounce, the toughest fighting fish on the planet. They are enthusiastic feeders so all you have to do is locate them and they will be waiting in line to get on your hook. Spawning beds are in shallow water near reeds and the best rig is a bobber 15–18 inches above a small hook baited with a bit of worm on 4–6 lb. test line.

You will have to fight the temptation to grab the line and "let me show you." Does it matter if one gets away? Be patient, isn't that one of fishing's lessons? Enjoy the setting and the excitement and then when you are done catching them, enjoy the bounty of your catch and eat them.

Bonding and bridging:

Catch and release is a wonderful idea to teach the children when they are young. This very simple idea encompasses sportsmanship and conservation, and children need to understand it early. The idea is that catching is the enjoyment and there will be no enjoyment if we harvest too many. We need to let the fish grow, reproduce, and keep the lake stocked. Taking the limit can be an exercise in greed.

Talk about greed, about conservation, about limited resources and making choices about what we need and what we want. These are important topics, but when you are having fun catching the bluegills and have to decide when its time to start putting them back, you have a perfect setting in which to explore the idea.

A word to the wise:

In 1985 Chicago set up an urban fishing program to introduce kids to fishing. Now a statewide program called Fish Illinois is a wonderful aid to you and your grandchildren. They hold clinics and also have over 160 locations with loaner fishing poles so that children can get started without a big expense. Try a clinic. They last about 2.5 hours and include both an instructional period and actual fishing at a nearby stocked lake.

Age of grandchild: 3 and up

Best season: Spring is really good for hungry and aggressive panfish

Contact:

I Fish Illinois; www.ifishillinois.org

Urban fishing program; www.ifishillinois.org/programs/Urban/urban.html

Kids and family fishing; www.ifishillinois.org/gofish/kids.htm

Also check out:

Kids Only Pond at Banner Marsh, Peoria County

Siloam Springs State Park Kid's Pond, Adams and Brown Counties

Gardening

There is both literal and figurative meaning when we suggest that you plant a garden with your grandchildren. All gardens begin with seeds and seeds are like magic capsules that hold all manner of life within them. As grandparents we have the ability to plant all kinds of philosophical and moral seeds in our grandchildren's minds. The fruit of this planting may not be seen for years to

come, but if planted with love and sincerity, it will bear fruit. Just think back to your own grandparents and see if you can't recognize traits or beliefs or abilities you carry today that they helped sow. This type of harvest could continue to grow through future generations, passing along the same kernels of wisdom. That is the philosophy of the garden.

A real garden is most practical for those who live relatively close to their grandchildren and can see them often enough to share and witness the growth of the vegetable or flower seeds they plant. It is not necessary to live in the country to do this together. Even those who live in city apartments can plant a few seeds in pots and watch the magic unfold. Every week there will be change. Caring for the plant as it grows can lead to lots of good discussion about what all living things need in order to prosper and survive. Little children love the opportunity to water plants, whether with a hose, watering can, or their own child size sprinkler.

If you have the space and ability to plant a full vegetable garden, they can help you stake out the rows and prepare the soil. Harvesting the crop is exciting and rewarding for all ages and it may just be one way to get that picky eater to try something they would never eat frozen or canned. Freshly picked, new carrots, with the dirt removed, taste nothing like the carrots you buy in the plastic bags from the grocery store, nor do freshly picked tomatoes. Many children today have little understanding of the food they eat, so growing even a single cherry tomato plant can be a revelation.

Bonding and bridging:

This activity doesn't have to end when the garden is put to bed in the fall, because in the middle of winter the seed catalogs arrive and you can sit down with the little ones, and go through all the colorful pages and begin to dream of next year's garden. Let them choose a variety of flowers and vegetables, maybe even making a small journal where they can cut and paste pictures of their choices and then they can record important information once the warm weather returns; such as when and what they planted, when the first sprouts appeared, how often they had to water or weed, what the weather was like, whether any bugs or animals ate their plants and when the flowers bloomed or the vegetables were picked. If you are working on math, you can count the plants and measure them. If you are working on the alphabet you can arrange the plantings by letter.

A word to the wise:

Sometimes boys can be harder to interest in the garden projects, but there are two things that will probably grab them—one is to plant a sunflower fort. You need a space large enough to plant a circle of sunflower seeds, so that when they grow up, they form an almost impenetrable living wall, a great place to hide out and make believe. A second activity guaranteed to provoke interest is a vermicompost system, a special variety of worms that create compost from your food scraps and other organic material. Observing the worms converting this material into soil, will elicit words like "cool" or maybe "gross," but it will be a source of fascination and a source of healthy new soil for your garden, too.

Age of grandchild: 3 to 12

Also check out:

University of Illinois Extension, Quincy; (217) 223-8380; http://web.extension.uiuc.edu/adamsbrown/hort_env.html

Illinois Garden site; www.gardensites.info/states/il.htm

Planning a children's garden; www.ehow.com/how_137652_design-children-garden.html

My First Garden, University of Illinois; www.urbanext.uiuc.edu/firstgarden

Morton Arboretum Children's Garden, Lisle; (630)968-0074; www.mortonarb.org/main.taf?p=2,1,2

Amtrak

I have always loved riding trains, ever since my mom took my brother and me on a trip to Chicago when I was about 8. The sound of the wheels clacking on the rails, the rocking of the cars, as if on the ocean, made it an adventure of grand proportions, even though we were only traveling from Minneapolis. Arriving and departing from depots with high marble ceilings added to the grandeur of the experience. There was glamour (the dining car) and wonder (the dome car at night) on those trips, and I have never lost the desire to ride the rails.

Luckily, in Illinois, there are still lots of options for train travel. Eight trains, with mythical names—the Illini, the Saluki, the Carl Sandburg, the Lincoln Service, and the Illinois Zephyr, the Empire Builder, and the Hiawatha service—can take you to over 30 cities. None are longer than five and a half hours, which is long enough to feel like a real trip, but don't require a sleeper or an overnight stay.

Today's children, especially little boys it seems, have a great fascination with one particular train—Thomas the Tank Engine. Maybe you remember the Lionel set you got for Christmas and played with for several years. Maybe you still have it and are ready to set it up again for a new generation of train buffs.

Riding the train today is a very comfortable experience. The seats are twice as roomy as those in airplanes and you can get up and walk around whenever you like – no seat belts. There are fold down tables and even electrical outlets near the seats, so you can plug in computers or other digital devices if you grow tired of watching the great scenery. And that has always been a big part of the pleasure of riding the train—traveling at a speed that allows us to see the landscape and the lives of the people we're passing. The trains go through backyards and industrial areas, past farmsteads and small towns. You can just barely hear the whistle in these well insulated cars, but it blows when you cross over some roads, with the warning arms down. Wave to the people who are standing by the side of the tracks or in their cars waiting for the train to pass; you are on a time machine.

Bonding and bridging:

Plan your train trip with your grandkids. Show them the choices of different routes and ask them where they'd like to go. Look up information about the destinations and find out what you can do in that town, before you catch the train back home. If you have a map to plot your trip on, use it to research the towns you will go through and bring it along to keep track of your progress.

Planning for a journey is half the fun and builds anticipation for the trip. Talk to the children about the way you traveled in the past and how it differs from today. Did your family have just one car? Encourage them to use their imagination to project how they will travel in 30 years.

A word to the wise:

Amtrak has had a reputation for being late, but they are working hard to correct this image. Part of it has to do with the availability of tracks, since freight trains often move on the same routes. With all the recent snafus and frustrations with air travel, trains are looking better all the time. At least you can get up and walk around and use the bathrooms on a train, even when you're not moving. Pack snacks or sandwiches for your trip, in case you are delayed. The Dining Car and Lounge Car serve food, but it is more expensive than you may want to pay. Bring along games to play too, since this is a great setting for conversation and one-on-one competition. The Lounge Car has domed windows and nice tables that you can sit at for game playing.

Age of grandchild: 3 and up

Best season: Any

Contact: Amtrak • (800) 872-7245 • www.amtrak.com

Also check out:

Monticello Railway Museum, Monticello; (217) 762-9011; www.mrym.org

Illinois Railroad Museum, Union; (815) 923-4000; www.irm.org

Fox River Trolley Museum. South Elgin; (847) 697-4676; www.foxtrolley.org

Campfire

What is it about a fire that is so pleasing when we sit outdoors at night or in a dark cabin in the fall or winter? Is this our most primitive instinct, some brain cells that connect us with our ancient cave dwelling ancestors? It is one of the basic ingredients to any good camping trip.

The Campfire Girls (now Camp Fire USA) explain their name on their website—"First meetings of Camp Fire Girls are held in Vermont [1910]. Dr.

Gulick chooses the name "Camp Fire" because campfires were the origin of the first communities and domestic life. Once people learned to make and control fire, they could develop and nurture a sense of community."

We are not sure if that is the true significance of campfires, but we have sat, stood, and enjoyed campfires in back country sites, at our home, and at the Audubon Center where we work. And we have never found anyone who does not relax in front of a crackling fire, in the smell of the smoke, and feeling of warmth. We agree with Thoreau's dictum on heating with fire and splitting wood: "they warmed me twice—once while I was splitting them, and again when they were on the fire, so that no fuel could give out more heat."

Teach your grandchildren that a good fire is a made of wood that is dry and not bigger than the size of the wrist. Engage the children in building and lighting the fire and let them learn to minimize their impact, while enjoying this natural pleasure. A good fire is not so large that you have to sit a long way off to avoid the heat. Make it the right size to light up your spot on earth; welcome everyone in close; and make it just big enough to provide heat, or cook a simple campfire food like the classic S'mores.

Campfires are a place for stories and conversation. Around the fire we lose perspective of who is speaking, which means that age, sex, and all the other things that work to separate us fall to the wayside. We become equals, sharing and listening to one another. The flames are mesmerizing and instead of relying on radio, TV, or videos, we become the source of ideas, images, and thoughts.

Bonding and bridging:

The fire seems safe because it provides light and warmth. We can cook on the fire and we can use it to communicate and share. These are strong bonding activities. In some ways the circle of light is like an invisible tent that encompasses everyone.

People have always felt safe at the fire, believing that wild animals will be kept at bay. Use the campfire to help your grandchildren fight night fears.

Have them face out from the fire, give time to let their eyes adjust, and then tell you what they see. Have them lay on the ground and adjust to the sky and the wonderful universe around them. If you are lucky you will hear different sounds and you can soothe them with the knowledge that these are not threatening, just the noise made by life in the dark.

A word to the wise:

State park campgrounds are a great place for a first camping experience and a nice campfire. But beware of one unfortunate fact. It is not good to bring wood from another locality, since we have now introduced so many pests from other continents that the wood we bring for warmth and cooking might be infested with something that could severely damage the wonderful location.

Age of grandchild: 2 and up

Best season: Summer

Contact:

A state park near you; Illinois Department of Natural Resources, Illinois State Parks; http://dnr.state.il.us/lands/landmgt/parks

Campfire story telling; www.netwoods.com/d-campfire.html

Campfire cooking; www.eartheasy.com/play_campfire_cooking.htm

Also check out:

A fireplace in your home, cabin, or resort

Your back yard barbeque or fire pit.

Shawnee National Forest; www.fs.fed.us/r9/forests/shawnee

The fire is the main comfort of the camp, whether in summer or winter, and is about as ample at one season as at another. It is as well for cheerfulness as for warmth and dryness. Henry David Thoreau

The Land of Poetry

Today's youth may think that the poets are dead and unimportant in the current world. Yet where would the world be without the great images that have formed today's literature or the poetry we set to music and call songs?

With a nod to the poet laureates Kevin Stein and Gwendolyn Brooks who deserve to be read and discussed, our adventure is better served in an active exploration between Galesburg and Springfield, with a journey on the Spoon River. Vachel Lindsay may be the least known of the three that we feature here, but in his day he was extremely popular and had a big public audience. Read

"The Mysterious Cat" with your young grandchild! Then visit the historic site where he lived. Read "Abraham Lincoln Walks at Midnight" when you visit Lincoln's tomb, in which Lindsay thinks of another Springfield resident.

> "It is portentous, and a thing of state
> That here at midnight, in our little town
> A mourning figure walks, and will not rest…"

Visit Carl Sandburg's humble home in Galesburg. His Lincoln biography won a Pulitzer prize. His poetry provided classic images like "Fog comes on little cat's feet" and his description of Chicago is still the best summary of the city's first century:

> "Hog Butcher of the World,
> Tool Maker, Stacker of Wheat,
> Player with Railroads and the Nation's Freight Handler;
> Stormy, husky, brawling,
> City of Big Shoulders."

And finally, canoe the Spoon River and share the poetry of Edgar Lee Masters. This wonderful river has become world-famous because of the poems named for it!

> "Life all around me here in the village:
> Tragedy, comedy, valor and truth,
> Courage, constancy, heroism, failure—
> All in the loom, and oh what patterns!"

And there you have the poetic adventure for three contemporaries of the "Chicago Group".

Bonding and bridging:

At Sandburg's home in April there are two events—the Songbag Folk Concerts that blends poetry and music, and the Sandburg Days Festival, which is a community celebration of their famous son. Poetry has always been the voice of protest and this is still true today. Far from being "difficult," this type of poetry is the voice of the people.

Take a book of poetry and read it aloud to your grandchildren. Then talk about the poems. Can you help your grandchild see Sandburg's "Fog" which "comes on little cat's feet?" If so, you can share the world of writing.

A word to the wise:

Another Illinois poet, Shel Silverstein, is perhaps the greatest poet of children's verse and his work is a great introduction to poetry. His books—*Where the Sidewalk Ends*, *A Light in the Attic*, and *The Giving Tree*—are classics. Buy them for the delightful word pictures as well as the wonderful art in the book. These are written for children and have the power to convey meaning in the lyrics.

Age of grandchild: 10 and up

Best season: Read in the winter, visit in the summer

Contact:

Vachel Lindsay Home, 603 South Fifth Street, Springfield, IL 62701
(217) 524-0901 • www.illinoishistory.gov/hs/vachel_lindsay.htm

Carl Sandburg Home 313 East Third Street, Galesburg, IL 61401
(309) 342-2361 • www.illinoishistory.gov/hs/carl_sandburg.htm

Edgar Lee Masters • www.poets.org/elmas

Spoon River • www.spoonriverdrive.org

Shel Silverstein poetry for kids • www.shelsilverstein.com

Also check out:

Your local library

Children are like windows that open onto the future as well as the past, the external world as well as our own private landscapes. Jane Swigart

Cemetery Visit

Grandparents have many important lessons to share. We suggest a visit to a cemetery even though this is hardly a typical experience.

For our grandchildren, our death may be the first great loss in their lives. I know that this is as hard to read as it is to write, but having lost a son, at age 21, in New Zealand, I also know that the weight of death is excruciatingly difficult. It is not necessary for us to have a "when I die" talk with our grandchildren, but we should let the fact of death be part of our life and that will make it easier.

Cemeteries have many lessons and it can be a good experience for you to be the one that helps them learn. We recommend choosing old cemeteries that reflect on history and events like the beautiful Calvary Cemetery, at Quincy, high on the banks of the Mississippi River with ancient oaks and a rolling landscape. One tree is famous as the Jesus Tree—but we will leave it to your imagination to determine if there really is an apparition here. We like the mix of graves from so many historic eras, the graves of founders and the graves of poor, the monument to the Civil War and the fact that it was constructed while the war was being fought not far from the area.

One more that we find intriguing is the Woodlawn Cemetery in Carbondale. The landscape is not as spectacular as Quincy's, but the stories are great. There is a memorial to the slaves who gained freedom, but succumbed to smallpox in 1864. There are Union soldier graves and Confederate too. And to really intrigue everyone there is the sarcophagus, a stone coffin that sits above ground.

We think of our cemeteries as lasting forever, but do they? We lost many of the burial grounds of the American Indian, due to insensitivity about the beliefs of the original Americans, but some such locations can still be found in the famous mound sites of Cahokia and Dickson Mounds. Near Sterling is Sinnissippi Park with its Hopewellian Indian Mounds overlooking the Rock River. Many Indian burial sites are still threatened by development.

Bonding and bridging:

If you visit cemeteries where people you knew are buried, you can relate to their stories. Even after our deaths, we live on in the photos, the stories, and the memories of our loved ones. This is why we should carry the stories of our family. It was the tradition of most societies without writing to orally share these stories from generation to generation. Now that we have books and writing, many people don't think about the stories to share through the spoken word, but how many families have books written about their experiences?

If you have created a family tree, this is a good time to share it. As weird as it sounds, this is where a family tree comes alive.

A word to the wise:

Bring a large piece of paper and chalk or charcoal. Place the paper over the old gravestones and put the chalk or charcoal on its side. Then rub it over the paper against the gravestone. The words and images should transfer without doing any damage to the gravestone. This can be taken home, a unique art project and a tool for recalling what you saw.

Age of grandchild: 10 and up

Also check out:

Graveyards of Chicago; www.graveyards.com

Oak Ridge Cemetery and Lincoln Tomb State Historic Site, Springfield; (217) 782-2717; http://showcase.netins.net/web/creative/lincoln/sites/tomb.htm

Illinois Cemetery Project; www.rootsweb.com/~ilsgs/ilcemetery.html

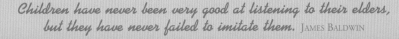

Children have never been very good at listening to their elders, but they have never failed to imitate them. JAMES BALDWIN

Farmers' Market

Maybe you've had the good fortune to travel to Europe and wander through the colorful, lively and fascinating outdoor markets. Almost every town or village has one day in the week when farmers come to town to sell their produce. It is a social occasion as well, where friends and neighbors meet and chat, and children chase one another around the legs of the adults.

I was lucky to have a grandmother who had been a farmer and when she moved to the city, a weekly trip to the Farmers' Market was her way to keep

that part of her past alive. As a child there were many Saturday mornings when I was roused from my bed at dawn to accompany my mother and grandmother to the Market. Any grumpiness I felt at this intrusion on my weekend was erased as soon as I smelled the ripe cantaloupe (or muskmelons as my grandmother called them).

In today's world very few children have the experience of caring for animals, picking food for the evening meal, or even running free in the pasture. A Farmers' Market with its colorful tables of produce, flowers, meats, and baked goods may be as close as many children will get to being at a farm, or meeting a farmer.

The best markets are hard to identify. The Amish country has a wonderful variety of vegetables in a quaint setting, while the Green City Market in Chicago includes great chefs demonstrating cooking, children's programs and a variety of garden presentations, as well as vendors with excellent produce.

There are so many lessons in this visit. Think about all of the contrasts between a Farmers' Market and supermarket, such as the packaging (or lack thereof). Also consider what healthy food is and what the word 'organic' means. At the Farmers' Market you can ask these questions of the people selling their vegetables and fruits.

Bonding and bridging:

It's easy to take food for granted. Whenever we want it, we know where to get it, the grocery store. Rarely do we consider "where does this food come from?"

A Farmers' Market is a chance to open your grandchild's eyes to the hard work and dedication that go into everything we eat. Tell him how important farmers are to our way of life. Share with him how difficult growing crops truly is and how we would struggle if there were no farmers to do this job. For older children, you may also want to bring up third-world countries in which food supplies are scarce. Either way, this is definitely a time when you want to help your grandchild learn to appreciate his every meal.

A word to the wise:

Ask your grandchild to think about what he'd like to have for lunch, and then make your visit finding the best ingredients—it can become a treasure hunt. Even the pickiest eater probably likes tomatoes, corn on the cob or watermelon. To complete the morning's excursion, let him choose a bouquet of freshly cut flowers to put on the table during your meal.

When you get home, let the child help clean the vegetables and prepare them for cooking. Explore the parts of the plant, the smells and textures, the taste and the variety. Keep them involved by cooking or eating at least one of the products and they might tell you when it's time to go to the next Farmers' Market.

Age of grandchild: All

Best season: Late spring, summer and early fall

Contact:

Illinois Department of Agriculture, PO Box 19281, Springfield, IL 62794 (217) 782-2172 • www.agr.state.il.us/markets/farmers/

Farmers' Market Online, Illinois Farmers Markets Directory www.farmersmarketonline.com/fm/Illinois.htm

Chicago's Green City Market, 2240 West Armitage, Chicago, IL 60647 (773) 435-0280 • www.chicagogreencitymarket.org

Library

Did you know that libraries are not an American invention or a creation of Mr. Carnegie? The Sumerians had a "House of Tablets"—imagine what it would have been like when everything was written on a clay tablet? The ancient Egyptians were the first to create a "House of Books" and they are credited with coming up with the form that would be the standard for books for the rest of civilization even though books themselves changed over time. First people invented the papyrus roll, certainly not as easy to store as books would be and then there was hieroglyphics, so that something could be put on the papyrus that would make sense. The earliest book was created in 4500 B.C.—the Book of the Dead, which began as a papyrus roll and later, appeared in book form. It was in Spain that the idea we take for granted came into use—putting books on shelves.

Our daughter Alyssa did her Master's in Library Science at Champagne Urbana, which has a wonderful heritage in library science. Having one of the great institutions for training librarians means that there are many great libraries for you to discover and the University of Illinois Library is the world's largest public university library!

In the U.S., one man—Andrew Carnegie—built 2,509 libraries between 1881 and 1917. His philanthropy was mostly in America, the British Isles and Canada. Open to the public, libraries have been one of the greatest successes for freedom of speech in the world. There were 106 Carnegie libraries in Illinois and the challenge is for you to search for those that remain.

Since that time, libraries have grown in many ways with over 4000 today in Illinois. All libraries are wonderful and offer great opportunities and treasures, but some also combine the excitement of an historic structure that means that the library is a story in and of itself. Such a library is the St. Charles Public Library, in St. Charles, IL. Built in the late 1930s the building attempted to capture the modern elements of its day. It includes an "eighty-four foot tall octagon tower, stained glass windows, pierced grillwork, and a diamond shaped translucent top" which makes the tower a scenic landmark. In Chicago, the Harold Washington Library with its gargoyle roofline and its children's library section is a terrific place to seek knowledge.

Be sure to explore the building, the exhibits and the programs as well as the books.

Bonding and bridging:

A fundamental goal of libraries is to instill in people (especially children) a lifelong love of reading and provide learning opportunities through books and various other media. Visiting a library together can foster a special relationship between the generations by bonding over the magic of a shared book. Grandparents have the patience to allow the child time to browse, to look and touch many volumes before making a choice, then bring a book home to share.

Perhaps the highlight of a grandchild's visit is that calm period of reading just before bed. It is a time when the book is a magical bridge between you and the grandchild, between generations and across imaginations.

A word to the wise:

Most libraries offer storytime when the librarians read selected books. This is a time when children share enthusiasm with one another. The readers use great voices and sounds, incorporate music and often movement to interact with the children, and the book becomes a magical device to connect everyone. Enabling this to happen is great, but it is important that you are there with them. By being attentive and participating, you show them that this wonderful experience is something you value too.

Age of grandchild: All

Best season: Any, but winter really seems the best time to bury oneself in the warmth and cozy atmosphere of a library.

Contact:

Illinois libraries • www.librarysites.info/states/il.htm

The Library History Buff • www.libraryhistorybuff.org/historylinks.htm

Chicago Public Library • www.chipublib.org

University Library, University of Illinois at Urbana-Champaign, 1408 West Gregory Drive, MC-522, Urbana, IL 61801 • www.library.uiuc.edu

Books are the treasured wealth of the world and the fit inheritance of generations and nations. HENRY DAVID THOREAU

Nature Centers

As culture becomes more complex we often lose the sense of place that was part of our ancestor's world. People used to connect with the land out of necessity through farming, logging, hunting, and fishing. Throughout the world the elders of the indigenous tribes state that everything they need is found in the land around them; that nature provides and they need to take care of nature It was a mutual respect and it worked.

Then we turned to industry and the cities and people became separated from the source of their food, their oxygen, their water. Naturalists offered people

insight through their writings and encouraged people to find inspiration and renewal by visiting natural areas, but this became a problem as the land became more and more developed. Around the time of the original Earth Day, the concept of the nature center took off. There are older centers, but the majority of what we call nature centers can date their history to that time and commitment.

Nature centers, unlike parks, were designed specifically to educate the user about the environment. They were created in neighborhoods and in the country. They emphasize forests or lakes or rivers or prairies. But most importantly they remind us that no matter how many stores we have, the basic goods still come from the earth, and we still need the clean air and water that nature provides.

Find a nature center near you and take your grandchild. on naturalist walks, sign up for classes that combine crafts and learning. Sit in on presentations and slide shows. Look at the exhibits and walk the trails. See the place in many seasons. Let them return so they know the people and the land and feel comfortable. It is a place where they can grow up with a sense of belonging to the land.

Many will have observation areas, maybe they will be making maple syrup, or raising bees. Some incorporate farm animals, others have wildlife blinds. The trails are good for walking in the summer, spring and fall and are often good places for cross country skis in the winter.

Bonding and bridging:

Many nature centers have benches where you can watch birds feed or look out on the forest, lake, or wetlands. These are good places for grandparent/grandchild sharing. What do they think is nature? Do they think people are part of nature?

What makes a place special? How does this place look to a bird or mammal? Is nature around their home and if so, can they watch it, enjoy it? What are the lessons they learned from visiting at the center? What did they like?

A word to the wise:

The nature center is a part of your neighborhood like a store, an office building, or a home. That implies that nature should be part of your community. Humans need to learn to live with other lifeforms, just as they adapt to the changes in our local setting. Building a good future for our grandchildren means allowing nature to have a role in our human communities.

Age of grandchild: All

Best season: Spring

Also check out:

Sand Ridge Nature Center, South Holland; (708) 868-0606; www.fpdcc.com

Vera Meineke Nature Center, Schaumberg; (847) 985-2100; www.parkfun.com/recreation/SpringValley/NatureCenter.aspx

Forest Park Nature Center, Peoria; (309) 686-3360; www.peoriaparks.org/fpnc/fpncmain.html

The Douglas-Hart Nature Center, Mattoon; (217) 235-4644; www.dhnature.org

Hawthorne Hill Nature Center, Elgin; (847) 931-6123; www.cityofelgin.org/index.asp?NID=564

Rock Springs Nature Center, Decatur; (217) 423-7708; www.maconcountyconservation.org/rocksprings.php

Index

A

Abraham Lincoln Presidential Library
and Museum 88–89
Adams County...139
Adler Planetarium & Astronomy
Museum 14–15, 31
Aerosport Management.......................................135
Air Classics Museum of Aviation 91
Air Festival..90
airplanes 20–21, 67, 90–91
Allis-Chalmers Museum...71
Alton...60, 65, 98, 99, 114
American Discovery Trail 104
American Farm Heritage Museum 71
American Girl Place 16–17, 97
Amish country 94–95, 127, 150
Amish Interpretive Center.....................................94
Amtrak..142–143
Anderson Japanese Gardens 54–55, 69
Anita Purvis Nature Center....................................93
Anna Bethel Fisher Rock Garden 55
Annual Rendezvous at Fort de Chartes 101, 113
Apple River Fort 101, 113
aquariums 24, 30–31, 32, 64–65, 99
Arcola.....................................73, 75, 94–95, 96-97
art 22–23, 25, 86–87, 93, 121, 147, 149
Arthur 73, 75, 94–95, 127
Arthur Cheese Festival 94
Arthur Days 94
Art Institute of Chicago, The.........................22–23
Ascension Ballooning Ltd. 135
Aurora...37
Aux Sable Aqueduct..60

B

bald eagles 114–115, 125
Bald Knob 107
Balloon Association of Greater Illinois 135
Banner Marsh 139
Barrington 25
baseball 40-41
Batavia 45, 135
Bay Creek 107
beaches 19, 20, 21, 78, 124, 136–137
Beardstown 83
bed and breakfasts...65
Belknap...108, 109
Bell Smith Springs 49
bicycling 18–19, 58, 60–61, 62, 104–105, 110, 116
Bike Chicago Rentals and Tours............................19
bird watching 44, 49, 108, 109, 114–115,
124, 155
Bishop Hill....................................72, 73, 75, 81, 95
Bloomington...............23, 29, 57, 77, 78, 79, 91, 120
boats..64, 65, 124, 127, 138
Bobby's Bike Hike...19
Bourbonnais 129
Bronzeville Children's Museum 25
Brookfield Zoo...29, 56, 77

Brown County 139
Buckingham Fountain 35
Burden Falls...107
Burpee Museum of Natural History.....27, 33, 52–53
Busey Woods 93

C

Cabin Festival 59
Cache River State Natural Area.............49, 104, 108,
109, 116
Cahokia 91
Cahokia Mounds State Historic Site 102–103, 148
Calvary Cemetery 148
campfires..58, 144–145
camping 107, 117, 145
Camp River Dubois...100
canoeing 108, 109, 116–117
Cantigny Park Sunday Outdoor Concert Series 47
Carbondale 33, 148
Carl Sandburg Home...................................146–147
Cave in the Rocks State Park 124
cemetery visits..................................58, 60, 148–149
Chain O'Lakes Area Artworks
Children's Museum 25
Chain O'Lakes State Park 125
Champaign 15, 33, 37, 152-153
Channahon State Park 60
Chanute Aerospace Museum 21, 67, 90–91
Charleston 83
Chester 111, 132, 133
Chester Gould Dick Tracy Museum, The 111
Chicago.................14–43, 45, 55, 57, 60, 77, 87, 89,
97, 120, 126-129, 133, 136-137, 139, 149-153
Chicago Air & Water Show 20–21, 136
Chicago Botanic Garden 42–43, 55, 69, 128
Chicago Children's Museum 24–25
Chicago City Pass 31
Chicago Cultural Center.......................................31
Chicago Gallery and Artisans Shop.......................87
Chicago History Museum 89
ChicagoKite 129
Chicago River 60
City of Giants State Park 124
Clarksville 114
Clay and Fiber Fest 73
Clear Springs Wilderness 107
Coal Valley...29, 57
Collinsville 102–103, 148
Confluence Bikeway 60
Contemporary Art Center....................................23
cooking 122–123, 145
Cypress Creek National Wildlife Refuge 108–109

D

Decatur 29, 55, 77, 115, 155
DeKalb 129
DeSoto House 62
Des Plaines 93
Des Plaines Conservation Area............................58

Dickson Mounds Museum 87, 103, 148
Discovery Center Museum..............................52–53
Dixon...63, 89
Dixon Springs...124
Doane Observatory..15
dolls...16–17, 96-97
Douglas-Hart Nature Center, The 155
Dresden Village Site...60
DuPage Children's Museum 25
DuPage River...116

E

East Moline...135
East St. Louis..35
Elgin 155
Elizabeth 101, 113
Elizabethtown 106, 107
Elmhurst Art Museum 23

F

farmers' markets....................................63, 150-151
Fern Clyffe State Park 124, 125
festivals..............45, 46-47, 59, 72, 73, 74, 90, 96-97,
    126, 129, 135, 147
Fever River Railroad Museum 51
Field Museum, The...................................26–27, 31
Firefly Pond Picnic Area....................................133
fireworks 126–127
Fish Illinois 139
fishing 60, 78, 124, 138–139
Forest City Hot Air Balloon................................135
Forest Park Nature Center 155
Fort de Chartes State Historic Site 101, 113
Fort Massac State Park 112–113
Fourth of July celebrations 126
Fox River 116, 125
Fox River Trolley Museum 51, 143
Franklin Creek State Natural Area 49
Franklin Grove...49
Freeport 51

G

Galena..62, 63
Galena River Trail 62
Galena State Historic Sites 63
Galesburg 51, 146, 147
Galesburg Railroad Museum................................51
Garden of the Gods 106–107
gardens 42–43, 54–55, 68–69, 92–93,
    106–107, 132, 133, 140–141
Garfield Park Conservatory..................................43
Gateway Geyser Fountain 35
Gaylord Building 60
Geneseo 126
Glencoe...42-43, 55, 69, 128
Glen Oaks Park..78, 79
Glenview 24-25
Godfrey..114
Goose Lake Prairie State Natural Area........49, 58–59
Grand Illinois Bike Trail....................................105
Grandparents Day...130–131

Granite City..114
Grant Park 34, 126
Greater St. Louis Air & Space Museum 91
Great River Road 115
Great River Trail..60–61
Green City Market.....................................150, 151
Greenville..71

H

Hanna City..76-77
Harold Washington Library 152, 153
Hartford 100-101
Harvest Festival..45, 72
Havana..103, 114
Hawthorne Hill Nature Center...........................155
Health World Children's Museum 25
Heidecke Fish and Wildlife Area........................58
Henry 114
Henry County 126
Heritage In Flight Museum...............................91
Highland Park 45, 46-47
hiking 44, 49, 60, 62, 69, 106, 108, 124
Hooppole..126
Hopewellian Indian Mounds 148
horseback riding...58
hot air balloon rides 134–135

I

Illinois and Indiana Antique Tractor and
    Gas Engine Club 71
I & M Canal Trail................................60–61, 116
Illinois Beach State Park 136-137
Illinois Farm Toy Show 17
Illinois Railway Museum.....................50–51, 143
Illinois Raptor Center 115
Illinois River 60, 98, 99, 114, 116, 125
Illlinois State Capitol 39, 84–85
Illinois State Military Museum............................67
Illinois State Museum....................23, 27, 86–87, 89
Illinois State Parks..124
Ingleside..25, 49

J

Jackson County..107
Jacksonville 71
Jim Hambrick Super Museum and Store 110-111
John Deere Pavilion 67, 68, 70–71
John Deere Tractor and Engine Factory 71
John G. Shedd Aquarium 30–31
John Hancock Building.................................38, 39
Julmarknad 73

K

Kankakee River 116
Kaskaskia 84, 85
Kids Only Pond 139
Kite Festival 129
kite flying...128–129
Kite Flying Contest..129
Klehm Arboretum..43, 69
Kohl Children's Museum 24-25

L

Lake Michigan........................60, 124, 128, 136–137
Lake Murphysboro State Park..............................124
Lakewood Museum of Arts and Science.................23
Laura Bradley Park...78, 79
Lerna...83
Lewis and Clark State Historic Site.............100–101
Lewistown..87, 103
libraries...88–89, 152–153
Lincoln..91, 135
Lincoln Courthouse...83
Lincoln-Douglas Debate Museum.........................83
Lincoln Home National Historical Site............82–83
Lincoln Log Cabin State Historic Site...................83
Lincoln Park...20, 21
Lincoln Park Zoo....................28–29, 32, 56, 57, 77
Lincoln's New Salem State Historic Site.....80–81, 83
Lincoln Tomb State Historic Site.........................149
Lisle..43, 55, 69, 141
living history.................................44, 80, 81, 101
Lockport...60, 87
Lockport Gallery..87
Lucia Nights...72
Lusk Creek Wilderness...107
Luthy Botanical Garden.......................................69

M

Macomb..33, 135
Manito..135
Mattoon..155
McCormick Tribune Plaza and Ice Rink.................35
McDonald's Cycle Center....................................19
McLean County Arts Center................................23
Meadowbrook Park..92–93
Melvin Price Dam...98, 999
Meredosia..114
Metropolis.............................110–111, 112, 113
Midewin National Tallgrass Prairie..................58–59
Midsommar Marque...72
Millenium Park..34–35
Miller Park Zoo............................29, 57, 77, 78–79
Mississippi Palisades State Park....................124, 125
Mississippi River..............60, 62, 64, 65, 69, 98, 99,
114, 115, 116, 124
Mississippi River Fish and Wildlife Area (MRA)....99
Missouri River..98
Moline...70, 71
Monticello Railway Museum.........................51, 143
Morris...49, 59, 61
Morton Arboretum.............43, 55, 69, 132, 133, 141
Museum of Geology, Western Illinois University ...33
Museum of Science and Industry.....................36-37
museums...............14–15, 24–27, 31, 33, 36–37, 45,
50–53, 66–67, 71, 83, 87-91, 98–99, 103, 110–111,
143, 148
music...45, 46-47, 72, 147

N

Naper Settlement..81
Naperville..25
National Great Rivers Museum.......60, 65, 98–99, 114

National Mississippi River Museum
and Aquarium.....................................31, 64–65, 99
National Toy Hall of Fame....................................97
nature centers.................44-45, 48-49, 58–59, 65, 104,
107, 108-109, 124, 154-155
Nature Institute, The..114
Nauvoo..73, 74–75, 95
Nauvoo Pageant...74
Navy Pier...21, 24, 126, 127
Niabi Zoo...29, 57, 69
North Avenue Beach..................................20, 21, 136
North Park Village Nature Center.........................45

O

Oak Ridge Cemetery...149
Oak Street Beach...20
Ohio River.................................98, 99, 108, 124
Old Chain of Rocks Bridge...................................114
Old Market House...62
Olive Park...20
Orion...126
Orpheum Children's Science Museum.............33, 37
Osaka Garden..55

P

Paris...71
parks, city.....20, 21, 34-35, 78-79, 92, 120–121, 128
parks, state..............60, 76, 112–113, 114, 124–125,
126, 133, 136, 137, 145
Peggy Notebaert Nature Museum, The..........32–33,
37, 45
Penfield...71
Peoria.....................15, 17, 23, 69, 78, 79, 120, 155
Peoria County..139
Pere Marquette State Park.............60, 114, 124, 125
Perry Farm Kite Festival.....................................129
Petersburg..80, 81, 83
Pfohl boat yards...65
P I Ball Balloons..135
Picnic in the Pasture..45
picnicking.........46, 47, 49, 60, 78, 92, 124, 132–133
planetariums...14–15
playgrounds...66, 92
poetry..146-147
Pontiac..135
Pope County...107
Popeye Picnic...132, 133
Popeye Statue...111
Prairie Aviation Museum.....................................91
Prairie du Rocher...101, 113
Prairie Land Heritage Museum.............................71
Prairie Ridge State Natural Area..........................109
Prophetstown...126

Q

Quad Cities.................................60, 68–69, 114
Quad City Botanical Center..........................68–69
Quincy...91, 114, 141, 148

R

Raggedy Ann & Andy Museum and
Festival..17, 96–97